A LIST OF

MASQUES, PAGEANTS, &c.

A LIST OF

MASQUES, PAGEANTS, &c.

SUPPLEMENTARY TO

A LIST OF ENGLISH PLAYS,

By WALTER WILSON GREG.

HASKELL HOUSE PUBLISHERS LTD.
Publishers of Scarce Scholarly Books
NEW YORK. N. Y. 10012
1969

First Published 1902

HASKELL HOUSE PUBLISHERS LTD.
Publishers of Scarce Scholarly Books
280 LAFAYETTE STREET
NEW YORK, N. Y. 10012

Library of Congress Catalog Card Number: 68-25312

Standard Book Number 8383-0942-9

Printed in the United States of America

PREFACE.

The present volume is put forward as a supplement to the *List of English Plays* issued in 1900. Besides an essay, in which I have sought to supply an introduction to the study of dramatic bibliography, both historical and technical, with appendices dealing with the antiquities of the subject, the volume includes a list of masques, pageants, entertainments, shows, and all such nondescript pieces as can make any pretence to dramatic form. The two volumes, therefore, together supply a survey of the whole of the English dramatic literature previous to the Civil War, which has come down to us in prints of the sixteenth and seventeenth centuries.

It will be readily imagined that the question as to what should and what should not be included was one which at times presented very considerable difficulties. The object being to illustrate as fully as possible the minor, less thoroughly and less formally, dramatic publications, the occurrence of speeches in character was taken as the test, provided they postulated some sort of scenic accompaniment, even though there was no evidence or even presumption of the piece having been actually represented. Thus mere dialogues, such as the innumerable eclogues, were excluded on the one hand, and the purely spectacular pageants and triumphs on the other. It was not, however, easy always to adhere to a hard and fast rule, and a certain number of exceptional cases had to be decided on their own merits. Three classes of works gave trouble in this respect. First, a certain

number of pageants, etc., included by previous writers on dramatic bibliography, were found to contain nothing dramatic whatever, but to be mere
descriptions of shows and triumphs. These have been, as a rule, omitted,
though I have, for the sake of completeness, made an exception of one or
two of Ben Jonson's entertainments, which strictly do not fulfil the test.
Secondly, we find a few genuinely dramatic pieces, of which, however,
nothing but the description or 'plot,' with perhaps a song or two is
preserved. These, too, since no essential dramatic portion is extant, have
been omitted. Lastly, there are certainly a number of poetical dialogues
which we know to have been actually recited in character and which are
yet entirely devoid of dramatic character. These likewise have been
omitted. A few examples of these three classes will be found in a note at
the end of this preface; I have made no attempt at giving a complete
collection.

The method upon which the titles have been transcribed and arranged
in the present list is identical with that previously adopted in compiling the
List of Plays in the Introduction to which all particulars will be found.
The work of transcription was carried out by Mr. H. Littlehales, but in
every case in which the original was accessible, I personally collated both
transcript and proof with it, and have spared no pains to make the *List* as
accurate as possible. I have much pleasure in acknowledging my indebtedness to Mr. R. B. McKerrow, who very kindly assisted in the arduous task
of compiling the appendix of early play lists.

I have taken this opportunity of printing a list of *Corrigenda* and
Addenda to my former volume, which I fear is a rather long one. In
excuse I can only state that, as previously explained, the *List of Plays* was
not published in the form originally intended, and some confusion occurred
through no one person being responsible for the final form, and also, I may

add, that in almost every case it has been left to me to detect the errors in my own work. Two acknowledgments only of a personal nature have I to make in this connection. It is with the greatest pleasure that I record my indebtedness to Professor Schick, who kindly pointed out to me the forgery included among the editions of *Solimon and Perseda*, and to Professor M. W. Sampson, of Indiana University, who has supplied me with various corrections in the transcripts.

Lastly, I wish to offer my thanks to Mr. A. W. Pollard, who has been ever ready with his assistance and advice, and to Mr. C. Sayle for much valuable help on some of the points of bibliography dealt with in the Essay Introductory, especially with regard to the highly important though little studied history of printers' devices.

WALTER WILSON GREG.

PARK LODGE, WIMBLEDON PARK,
January, 1902.

NOTE.

The specimens of works excluded from the present list, to which allusion has been made above, are as follows :

(i.)   Pageants, etc., included by previous compilers :

The Passage of our most drad Soueraigne Lady Quene Elyzabeth through the citie of London to westminster the daye before her coronacion. *Richard Tottill,* 1558.

[Another edition.]   *S. S. for Ione Millington.*   1604.

[Another issue.]   *S. S. for Iohn Busby.*

Polyhymnia. Describing, The honourable Triumph at Tylt, before her Maiestie, on the 17. of Nouember last past.   [By George Peele.] *Richard Jhones.*   1590.

King Iames his entertainment at Theobalds : With his Welcome to London. By John Sauile. *Thomas Snodham, T. Este.* 1603.

The Time Triumphant, describing the arrival of King Iames into England, and his Coronation at Westminster. [By Gilbert Dugdale.] *R. B.* 1604.

The Most royall entertainement of Christiern the fourth, King of Denmarke. By H. R[oberts]. *for H. R. by William Barley,* 1606.

Englands Farewell to Christian the fourth, famous King of Denmarke. By H. Roberts. *for William Welby.* 1606.

The Triumphs Of The Golden Fleece. By A. Mundy. *T. S.* 1623.

Englands Comfort, and Londons Ioy : Expressed in the Entertainment of King Charles. [By John Taylor.] *for Francis Coules.* 1641.

The solempnities & triumphes at the Mariage of the Ladye Marye. *R. Pynson.* [1507.]

Jousts of the Months of May and June. [W. de Worde or R. Pynson. 1508.]

The maner of the tryumph at Caleys and Bulleyn. [1532.]

[Another edition.] The second pryntyng. [1532.]

(ii.)   Descriptions of dramatic performances :

The Argument of the Pastorall of Florimene, with the Description of the Scenes and Intermedij. *for Thomas Walkley.* 1635.

Masquarade du Ciel : Presented to the Great Queene of the Little World. A Celestiall Map, representing The True Site and Motions of the Heavenly Bodies, through the yeeres 1639, 1640, &c. By J. S[adler]. *R. B. for S. C.* 1640.

Princeps Rhetoricus or Πιλομαχία· yᵉ Combat of Caps. Drawn forth into Arguments, General and Special. [By John Mason.] *for H. R.* 1648.

(iii.)   Dialogues recited in character :

A Contention betwixt a Wife, a Widow and a Maide.   By Sir Iohn
Davies.   In Davison's *Poetical Rhapsody*, 1608, etc.

A Dialogue between two Shepherds, Thenot and Piers, in Praise of
Astrea.   Made by the excellent Lady, the Lady Mary Countess of
Pembroke, at the Queen Majesty's being at her home at———,
Anno 15**.   In Davison's *Poetical Rhapsody*, 1602, etc.

A Dialogue betweene two Shephards, vttered in a pastorall shew at
Wilton.   By Sir Philip Sidney.   In the *Arcadia*, 1598, etc.

LIST OF MASQUES, PAGEANTS, &c.

AMERIE, ROBERT. (*fl.* 1610.)

Chesters Triumph in Honor of her Prince. As it was performed vpon
S. Georges Day 1610. in the foresaid Citie. *for I. B.* 1610.

> The name of the author appears at the end.
>
> R. Davies, to whom Hazlitt ascribes the piece, only contributed one poem and the
> prefatory matter.
>
> B.M. (C. 30. d. 3.) Bodl.

BEAUMONT, FRANCIS, and **FLETCHER, JOHN.** (1584–1616 and
1597–1625.)

Comedies and Tragedies . . . . 1647. Fol.

> See *Plays*, p. 3. Contains the masque with head-title at sig. *8 D 2, as follows:
>
> The Maske of the Gentlemen of Grayes-Inne, and the Inner-Temple, Performed
> before the King in the Banqueting-house at White-hall, at the marriage of the
> Illustrious Frederick and Elizabeth, Prince and Princesse Palatine of the Rhene.
> Written by Francis Beamont Gentleman.

Fifty Comedies and Tragedies. . . . . M.D.CLXXIX. Fol.

> See *Plays*, p. 4. Contains the masque with head-title similar to above at sig. 3 X 3.

---

*The Masque of the Inner Temple and Grayes Inne: Grayes Inne and the
Inner Temple, presented before his Maiestie, the Queenes Maiestie, the
Prince, Count Palatine and the Lady Elizabeth their Highnesses, in the
Banquetting house at White-hall on Saturday the twentieth day of
Februarie, 1612. *F. K. for George Norton.*

> B.M. (C. 34. e. 57.)

[Another issue.] By Francis Beaumont, Gent. *F. K. for George
Norton.*

> The sheets of the above issued with a different titlepage.

CAMPION, THOMAS. (d. 1619.)

The Discription of a Maske, Presented before the Kinges Maiestie at White-
Hall, on Twelfth Night last, in honour of the Lord Hayes, and his Bride,

B

Daughter and Heire to the Honourable the Lord Dennye, their Marriage hauing been the same Day at Court solemnized. To this by occasion other small Poemes are adioyned. Inuented and set forth by Thomas Campion Doctor of Phisicke. *John Windet for John Brown.* 1607.

> An engraving on the verso of titlepage.
> The music to the songs is given at the end.
>
> B.M. (C. 21. c. 43.) Bodl.

A Relation of the late royall Entertainment giuen by the Right Honorable the Lord Knowles, at Cawsome-House neere Redding : to our most Gracious Queene, Queene Anne, in her Progresse toward the Bathe, vpon the seuen and eight and twentie dayes of Aprill. 1613. Whereunto is annexed the Description, Speeches, and Songs of the Lords Maske, presented in the Banquetting-house on the Mariage night of the High and Mightie, Count Palatine, and the Royally descended the Ladie Elizabeth. Written by Thomas Campion. *for John Budge.* 1613.

> The *Lords' Masque* has a separate head-title on sig. C1.
>
> In some copies, as for instance C. 33. e. 7. (8), the author's name appears as "Campian" on the titlepage.
>
> B.M. (C. 21. c. 48. and C. 33. e. 7. (8)). Bodl.

The Description of a Maske : Presented in the Banqueting roome at White-hall, on Saint Stephens night last, At the Mariage of the Right Honourable the Earle of Somerset : And the right noble the Lady Frances Howard. Written by Thomas Campion. Whereunto are annexed diuers choyse Ayres composed for this Maske that may be sung with a single voyce to the Lute or Base-Viall. *E. A. for Laurence Li'sle.* 1614.

> This is the *Squires' Masque*. The music is given at the end.
>
> B.M. (C. 34. c. 7.) Bodl.

CAREW, THOMAS. (1598 ?–1639 ?)

Poems. By Thomas Carew Esquire. One of the Gentlemen of the Privie-Chamber, and Sewer in Ordinary to His Majesty. *I. D. for Thomas Walkley.* 1640. 8vo.

> Contains the masque with separate titlepage at sig. O8, as follows :
>
> Cœlum Brittanicum. A Masque at White-Hall in the Banquetting house, on Shrove-Tuesday-night, the 18. of February, 1633. The Inventors, Tho. Carew. Jnigo Iones. *for Thomas Walkley.* 1640.
>
> B.M. (11623. aaa. 5.) T.C.C.

[Another edition.] The second Edition revised and enlarged. *I. D. for Thomas Walkley.* 1642. 8vo.

> Contains the masque with separate titlepage at sig. P2, as before, with imprint dated 1642.
>
> B.M. (1077. b. 25.)

Poems, With a Maske, by Thomas Carew Esq; One of the Gent. of the Privy-Chamber, and Sewer in Ordinary to his late Majestie. The Songs were set in Musick by Mr. Henry Lawes Gent. of the Kings Chappell, and one of his late Majesties Private Musick. The third Edition revised and enlarged. *for H. M. sold by J: Martin.* 1651. 8vo.

> Contains the masque with separate titlepage at sig. L7, bearing the imprint: *for Hum. Moseley.* 1651.
>
> B.M. (643. a. 17.) Bodl.

Poems, Songs and Sonnets, Together with a Masque. By Thomas Carew Esq; One of the Gentlemen of the Privy-Chamber, and Sewer in Ordinary to His late Majesty. The Songs set in Musick by Mr. Henry Lawes, Gentleman of the Kings Chappel, and one of His late Majesties Private Musick. The Fourth Edition revised and enlarged. *for Henry Herringman.* 1670. 8vo.

> Contains the masque with separate titlepage at sig. M3, bearing the imprint: *In the Savoy, for Henry Herringman,* 1670.
>
> Dyce.

[Another issue.] *for H. Herringman, sold by Hobart Kemp,* 1671. 8vo.

> The sheets of the above re-issued with a new titlepage. It is said that in some copies the date of the masque is likewise altered.
>
> B.M. (1076. g. 11.)

The Works of Sr William Davenant Kt . . . . . 1673.

> *Vide infra.*

---

*Cœlum Britanicum. A Masque at White-Hall in the Banquetting-house, on Shrove-Tuesday-night, the 18. of February, 1633. *for Thomas Walkley.* 1634.

> B.M. (1103. e. 70.) Bodl. U.L.C.

CHAPMAN, GEORGE. (1569–1634.)

The memorable Masque of the two honourable Houses or Innes of Court; the Middle Temple, and Lyncolnes Inne. As it was performed before the

King, at White-hall on Shroue-Munday at night; being the 15. of Febr. 1613. At the princely Celebration of the most royall Nuptialls of the Palsgraue, and his thrice gratious Princesse Elizabeth, &c. With a description of their whole show, in the manner of their march on horse backe to the Court, from the Master of the Rolls his house: with all their right Noble consorts, and most showfull attendants. Inuented, and fashioned, with the ground, and speciall structure of the whole worke: By our Kingdomes most Artfull and Ingenious Architect Innigo Iones. Supplied, Applied, Digested, and written, By Geo. Chapman. *F. K. for George Norton.*

> B.M. (C. 34. b.)

[Another edition.] *G. Eld, for George Norton.*

> B.M. (C. 34. c. 56.) Bodl. U.L.C.

CHURCHYARDE, THOMAS. (1520?–1604.)

A Discourse of The Queenes Maiesties entertainement in Suffolk and Norffolk : With a description of many things then presently seene. Deuised by Thomas Churchyarde, Gent. with diuers shewes of his own inuention sette out at Norwich : and some rehearsal of hir Highnesse retourne from Progresse. Wherevnto is adioyned a commendation of Sir Humfrey Gilberts ventrous iourney. *Henrie Bynneman.* Partly 𝕭.𝕷.

> B.M. (G. 11,238.) Bodl.

COCKAYNE, SIR ASTON. (1608–1684.)

A Chain of Golden Poems. . . . . 1658. 8vo.

> See *Plays*, p. 22. This and the subsequent issues contain, with head-title at sig. I 3ᵛ :
>
> A Masque Presented at Bretbie in Darbyshire On Twelfth-Night. 1639.

DANIEL, SAMUEL. (1563–1619.)

The Whole Works of Samuel Daniel. . . . . 1623.

> See *Plays*, p. 26. This and the re-issue of 1635 contain the *Vision* with separate titlepage at sig. 2 O 8, as follows :
>
> The Vision of the Twelue Goddesses, presented in a Maske the eight of January, at Hampton Court. By the Queenes most excellent Maiesty, and her Ladies. By Samuel Daniel. *Nicholas Okes, for Simon Waterson.* 1623.

---

*[The Vision of the Twelue Goddesses.] The true discription of a Royall Masque. Presented at Hampton Court, vpon Sunday night, being the eight

of Ianuary. 1604. And Personated by the Queenes most Excellent Majestie, attended by Eleuen Ladies of Honour. *Edward Allde.* 1604.

> An unauthorised edition of the *Vision.*

> B.M. (C. 33. e. 7 (21).) Bodl.

The Vision of the 12. Goddesses, presented in a Maske the 8. of Ianuary, at Hampton Court: By the Queenes most excellent Maiestie, and her Ladies. *T. C. for Simon Waterson.* 1604. 8vo.

> The author's name appears at the end of the epistle dedicatory.

> Bodl.

The Order and Solemnitie of the Creation of the High and mightie Prince Henrie, Eldest Sonne to our sacred Soueraigne, Prince of Wales, Duke of Cornewall, Earle of Chester, &c. As it was celebrated in the Parliament House, on Munday the fourth of Iunne last past. Together with the Ceremonies of the Knights of the Bath, and other matters of speciall regard, incident to the same. Whereunto is annexed the Royall Maske, presented by the Queene and her Ladies, on Wednesday at night following. *for Iohn Budge.* 1610.

> The separate titlepage to the masque at sig. D4 runs:

> Tethys Festiual: or the Queenes Wake. Celebrated at Whitehall, the fifth day of June 1610. Deuised by Samuel Daniel, one of the Groomes of her Maiesties most Honourable priuie Chamber. *for Iohn Budge.* 1610.

> B.M. (C. 33. e. 7 (12).) Bodl. U.L.C. Dyce.

D'AVENANT, SIR WILLIAM. (1606–1668.)

The Works of Sr William Davenant K^t . . . . 1673.

> See *Plays,* p. 27. Contains, among "Poems on several Occasions," at 2 U 4, the *First Day's Entertainment at Rutland House,* at 3 B 4^v the *Temple of Love,* and at 3 D 3 the *Triumphs of the Prince D'Amour;* also at 2 Z 1^v Carew's *Cœlum Britannicum,* each with head-title only.

The Temple of Love. A Masque. Presented by the Queenes Majesty, and her Ladies, at White-hall on Shrove-Tuesday, 1634. By Inigo Iones, Surveyour of his Majesties Workes; and William Davenant, her Majesties Servant. *for Thomas Walkley.* 1634.

> B.M. (C. 21. c. 35 (7).) Bodl.

The Triumphs of the Prince d'Amour. A Masque presented by His Highnesse at His Pallace in the Middle Temple, the 24th of Februarie 1635.
for Richard Meighen. 1635.

> The author's initials appear at the end of the epistle to the reader.
>
> B.M. (C. 33. d. 12.) U.L.C.

Britannia Triumphans: a Masque, Presented at White Hall, by the Kings
Majestie and his Lords, on the Sunday after Twelfth-night, 1637. By
Inigo Iones Surveyor of his Majesties workes, and William Davenant her
Majesties servant. *Iohn Haviland for Thomas Walkley*, 1637.

> B.M. (C. 34. c. 57.)

Salmacida Spolia. A Masque. Presented by the King and Queenes Majesties, at White-hall, On Tuesday the 21. day of January 1639. *T. H. for
Thomas Walkley.* 1639.

> In a note at the end occurs the statement " What was spoken or sung, [was made]
> by William Davenant, her Majesties Servant."
>
> B.M. (644. d. 65.) Bodl.

The first days Entertainment at Rutland-House, By Declamations and
Musick: After the manner of the Ancients. By Sr W. D. *J. M. for
H. Herringman.* 1657. 8vo.

> B.M. (E. 1648 (2), dated by Thomason, "Nov. 22. 1656.") Bodl.

*The Cruelty of the Spaniards in Peru. Exprest by Instrumentall and Vocall
Musick, and by Art of Perspective in Scenes, &c. Represented daily at the
Cockpit in Drury-Lane At Three after noone punctually. *for Henry
Herringman.* 1658.

> Afterwards formed part of the *Playhouse to Let.* (See *Plays*, p. 27.)
>
> B.M. (644. d. 69.) Bodl.

*The History of Sr Francis Drake. Exprest by Instrumentall and Vocall
Musick, and by Art of Perspective in Scenes, &c. The First Part.
Represented daily at the Cockpit in Drury-Lane at Three Afternoon
Punctually. *for Henry Herringman.* 1659.

> Afterwards formed part of the *Playhouse to Let.* (See *Plays*, p. 27.)
>
> B.M. (644. d. 70.) Bodl.

DAY, JOHN. (*fl.* 1606.)

The Parliament of Bees, With their proper Characters. Or A Bee-hive
furnisht with twelve Honycombes, as Pleasant as Profitable. Being an

Allegoricall description of the actions of good and bad men in these our daies. By John Daye, Sometimes Student of Caius Colledge in Cambridge. *for William Lee.* 1641.

> With woodcut facing title.
>
> B.M. (C. 34. c. 21.)

DEKKER, THOMAS. (1570?–1641?)

The magnificent Entertainment : Giuen to King Iames, Queene Anne his wife, and Henry Frederick the Prince, vpon the day of his Maiesties Tryumphant Passage (from the Tower) through the Honourable Citie (and Chamber) of London, being the 15. of March. 1603. As well by the English as by the Strangers : With the speeches and Songes, deliuered in the seuerall Pageants. Tho. Dekker. *T. C. for Tho. Man the yonger.* 1604.

> One of the speeches was written by Middleton.
>
> B.M. (C. 24. c. 23.) Bodl. Dyce.

[Another edition.] *Edinburgh, Thomas Finlason.* 1604. *with Licence.*

> B.M. (C. 33. d.).

The Whole Magnifycent Entertainment : Giuen to King James, Queene Anne his wife, and Henry Frederick the Prince ; vpon the day of his Majesties Tryumphant Passage (from the Tower) through his Honorable Citie (and Chamber) of London, the 15. of March. 1603. Aswell by the English, as by the Strangers, with the speeches and Songs, deliuered in the seuerall Pageants. And those speeches that before were publish't in Latin, now newly set forthe in English. Tho. Dekker. *E. Allde for Tho. Man the yonger.* 1604.

> Bodl. T.C.C.

Troia-Noua Triumphans. London Triumphing, or, The Solemne, Magnificent, and Memorable Receiuing of that worthy Gentleman, Sir Iohn Swinerton Knight, into the Citty of London, after his Returne from taking the Oath of Maioralty at Westminster, on the Morrow next after Simon and Iudes day, being the 29. of October. 1612. All the Showes, Pageants, Chariots of Triumph, with other Deuices, (both on the Water and Land) here fully exprcssed. By Thomas Dekker. *Nicholas Okes, sold by Iohn Wright.* 1612.

> B.M. (C. 33. e. 7. (17).) Bodl.

Brittannia's Honor : Brightly Shining in seuerall Magnificent Shewes or Pageants, to Celebrate the Solemnity of the Right Honorable Richard

Deane, At his Inauguration into the Majoralty of the Honourable Citty of London, on Wednesday, October the 29th. 1628. At the particular Cost, and Charges of the Right Worshipfull, Worthy, and Ancient Society of Skinners. Inuented by Tho. Dekker. *Nicholas Okes and Iohn Norton,* 1628.

         B.M. (C. 33. e. 7. (10).)

London's Tempe, or, The Feild of Happines. In which Feild are planted seuerall Trees of magnificence, State and Bewty, to celebrate the Solemnity of the Right Honorable James Campebell, at his Inauguration into the Honorable Office of Prætorship, or Maioralty of London, on Thursday the 29. of October, 1629. All the particular Inuentions for the Pageants, Showes of Triumph, both by Water and Land, being here fully set downe. At the sole Cost, and liberall Charges of the Right worshipful Society of Ironmongers. Written by Thomas Dekker.

         Devon. Rowfant.

GARTER, Bernard. (*fl.* 1570.)

The Ioyfull Receyuing of the Queenes most excellent Maiestie into hir Highnesse Citie of Norwich : The things done in the time of hir abode there : and the dolor of the Citie at hir departure. Wherein are set downe diuers Orations in Latine, pronounced to hir Highnesse by Sir Robert Wood Knight, now Maior of the same Citie, and others : and certaine also deliuered to hir Maiestie in writing : euery of thē turned into English. *Henrie Bynneman.* Partly 𝕭.𝕷.

     The author's, or rather compiler's, abbreviated name, "Ber. Gar." occurs in the Dedication. It was, however, partly written by Henry Goldingham.
         B.M. (C. 33. e. 7. (2) (impf.). Bodl.

GASCOIGNE, George. (1525 ?–1577.)

A Hundreth sundrie Flowres . . . . . . [n.d.]

     See *Plays,* p. 39. The "deuise of a maske for the right honorable Viscount Mortacute" occurs at sig. 2A3^v.

The Posies of George Gascoigne Esquire . . . . . [1575].

     See *Plays,* p. 40. The *Device of a Masque* occurs at sig. C6.

The Whole woorkes of George Gascoigne Esquyre . . . 1587.

     See *Plays,* p. 40. The *Device of a Masque* occurs at sig. C6., and the *Princely Pleasures at Kenelworth* at sig A1 (fourth register).

*The Princelye pleasures, at the Courte at Kenelwoorth. That is to saye. The Copies of all such verses Proses, or Poeticall inuentions, and other Deuices of pleasure, as were there deuised, and presented by sundry Gentle men, before the Quenes Maiestie: In the yeare 1575. *Rychard Ihones.* 1576. 8vo.

> Haz. H. 222. Also facsimile reprint of titlepage in Hazlitt's edition of Gascoigne in the Roxburghe Library, 1870, from a tracing by Halliwell-Phillipps. The only known copy was sold in the Farmer sale in 1798, and ultimately found its way to the Midland Institute. (Haz. I. 179). It was presumably burnt in the fire at the Shakespear Library at Birmingham. (Haz. II. 695).

*[The Queenes Majesties Entertainement at Woodstock.] [Colophon :] *for Thomas Cadman.* 1585.

> Imperfect, wanting sig. A; Hermits Tale of Contarenus and Caudina, by Gascoigne, B–B3; Play, on same subject, probably also by Gascoigne, C3–G3. The only copy known.
>
> Rowfant.

GOLDWELL, HENRY. (*fl.* 1580.)

A briefe declaratiō of the shews, deuices, speeches, and inuentions, done & performed before the Queenes Maiestie, & the French Ambassadours, at the most valiaunt and worthye Triumph, attempted and executed on the Munday and Tuesday in Whitson weeke last, Anno 1581 Collected, gathered, penned & published, by Henry Goldwel, Gen. *Robert Walde-grave.* 8vo. partly 𝔅.𝔏.

> B.M. (C. 33. a. 4).

HEYWOOD, THOMAS. (1575?-1650?)

Pleasant Dialogues and Dramma's, selected out of Lucian, Erasmus, Textor, Ovid, &c. With sundry Emblems extracted from the most elegant Iacobus Catsius. As also certaine Elegies, Epitaphs, and Epithalamions or Nuptiall Songs; Anagrams and Acrosticks; With divers Speeches (upon severall occasions) spoken to their most Excellent Majesties, King Charles, and Queene Mary. With other Fancies translated from Beza, Bucanan, and sundry Italian Poets. By Tho. Heywood. *R. O. for R. H. sold by Thomas Slater* 1637. 8vo.

> The last three of the dialogues alone are dramatic, *viz. Iupiter and Io* at sig. L6, *Apollo and Daphne* at N1, and *Amphrissa, the forsaken Shepherdess,* or *Pelopœa and Alope* at N8ᵛ.
>
> B.M. (1076. i. 29.) Bodl. U.L.C. T.C.C.

Londons Ius Honorarium. Exprest in sundry Triumphs, pagiants, and shews,
   At the Initiation or Entrance of the Right Honourable George Whitmore,
   into the Maioralty of the famous and farre renowned Citty of London.   All
   the charge and expence of the laborious proiects and obiects both by
   Water and Land, being the sole vndertaking of the Right Worshipfull, the
   Society of the Habberdashers.   [Woodcut]   *Nicholas Okes.*   1631.

> The author's name appears at the end of two epistles dedicatory.   On the titlepage
> is a woodcut of the Haberdashers' arms.
>
> Bodl.

Londini Artium et Scientiarum Scaturgio.   Londons Fountain of Arts and
   Sciences; exprest in sundrie Triumphes, Pageants and Shews, at the
   Initiation of the Right Honorable Nich. Raynton, in the Majoralty of the
   famous and far-renowned City of London.   All the Charge and Expense of
   the Laborious Projects, both by Sea and Land, being the sole Undertaking
   and Charge of the Right Worshipfull Company of Haberdashers.   Written
   by Thomas Heywood.   1632.

> Haz.   H. 272.

Londini Emporia, or Londons Mercatura : exprest in sundry triumphs,
   pageants, and showes, at the inauguration of the Right Honorable Ralph
   Freeman into the Maioralty of the famous and farre-renowned citty London.
   All the charge and expense of the laborious proiects, both by water and
   land being the sole undertaking of the Right Worshipfull Company of the
   Cloath-workers.   Written by Thomas Heywood.   *Nicholas Okes.*   1633.

> Haz.   H. 272.

Londini Sinus Salutis, or, Londons Harbour of Health, and Happinesse.
   Epressed [*sic*] in sundry Triumphs, Pageants, and Showes ; at the Initiation
   of the Right Honorable, Christopher Clethrowe, Into the Maioralty of the
   farre Renowned City London.   All the Charges and Expences of this
   present Ovation ; being the sole undertaking of the Right Worshipfull
   Company of the Ironmongers.   The 29. of October. Anno Salutis. 1635.
   Written by Thomas Heywood.   *Robert Raworth.*   1635.   8vo.

> The copy in the Bright sale of 1845 (Haz. H. 273), though stated to be in 4to, was
> no doubt in reality of the same edition.   There is a woodcut of the Ironmongers'
> arms on the verso of the titlepage.
>
> Dyce.

Londini Speculum : or, Londons Mirror, Exprest in sundry Triumphs,
   Pageants, and Showes, at the Initiation of the right Honorable Richard
   Fenn, into the Mairolty of the Famous and farre renowned City London.

All the Charge and Expence of these laborious projects both by Water and Land, being the sole undertaking of the Right Worshipful Company of Habberdashers.   Written by Tho. Heywood.   [Woodcut.]   *I. Okes.* 1637.

> A woodcut of the Haberdashers' arms appears on the titlepage.
>
> Bodl.

Porta pietatis, or, The Port or Harbour of Piety.   Exprest in sundry Triumphes, Pageants, and Showes, at the Initiation of the Right Honourable Sir Maurice Abbot Knight, into the Majoralty of the famous and farre renowned City London.   All the charge and expence of the laborious Projects both by water and Land, being the sole undertaking of the Right Worshipfull Company of the Drapers.   Written by Thomas Heywood.   *I. Okes.* 1638.

> B.M. (113. l. 10.)   Bodl.

Londini Status Pacatus : or, Londons Peaceable Estate.   Exprest in sundry Triumphs, Pageants, and Shewes, at the Innitiation of the right Honourable Henry Garway, into the Majoralty of the Famous and farre Renowned City London.   All the Charge and Expence, of the laborious Projects both by Water and Land, being the sole undertakings of the Right Worshipfull Society of Drapers.   Written by Thomas Heywood.   *Iohn Okes.* 1639.

> B.M. (C. 30. d. 12.)   Bodl.

JONSON, BENJAMIN. (1573?-1637.)

The Workes of Beniamin Jonson . . . . 1616.

> See *Plays*, p. 55.   Contains at sig. 4B and following, these masques (Gifford's titles are added in brackets) :
>
> Part of the Kings Entertainment in passing to his Coronation.
>
> A Particular Entertainment of the Queene and Prince their Highnesse at Althrope, at The Right Honourable the Lord Spencers, on Satturday being the 25. of Iune 1603.
> [*The Satyr.*]
>
> > These two have separate titlepages with the imprint : *London*, M.DC.XVI.
>
> A Priuate Entertainment of the King and Queene, on May-day in the Morning, At Sir William Cornwalleis his house, at High-gate.   1604.
> [*The Penates.*]
>
> The entertainment of the two Kings of Great Brittaine and Denmarke at Theobalds, Iuly 24. 1606.

An Entertainment of King Iames and Queene Anne, at Theobalds, ... 22. of May, 1607.
> These have only head-titles.

Masques at Court.   *London*, M.DC.XVI.

> Separate titlepage to the following masques, each of which has head title only :

The Queenes Masques.   The first, of Blacknesse : Personated at the Court, at White-Hall, on the Twelu'th night, 1605.

The Second Masque.   Which was of Beautie ; Was presented in the same Court, at White-Hall, on the Sunday night after the Twelfth Night.   1608.

Hymenæi, or The solemnities of Masque and Barriers at a Marriage.

The Description of the Masque.   With the Nuptiall songs.   At the Lord Vicount Hadingtons marriage at Court.   On the Shroue-tuesday at night. 1608.   [*The Hue and Cry after Cupid.*]

The Masque of Queenes, ... At White-Hall.   Febr. 2. 1609.

The Speeches at Prince Henries Barriers.

Oberon, the Faery Prince.   A Masque of Prince Henries.

A Masque of her Maiesties.   Love freed from Ignorance and Folly.

Love Restored, In a Masque at Court.

A Challenge at Tilt, at a Marriage.

The Irish Masque at Court.

Mercury Vindicated from the Alchemists at Court.

The Golden Age Restor'd.   In a Maske at Cour', 1615.

The Workes of Benjamin Jonson . . . . 1640.

> See *Plays*, p. 55.   Contains, at sig. F4 (second register) and following, the same masques as above, with following variations :—
>> All separate title pages, as above, have imprint : *London, Printed by Richard Bishop*, M.DC.XL.
>> Love Freed from Ignorance and Folly.   A Masque of Her Maiesties.

The Workes of Benjamin Jonson.   The second volume . . . . . 1640.

> See *Plays*, p. 55–6.   Contains at sig. B (third register) and following, these masques (Gifford's titles in brackets as before) :
>> Christmas, his Masque ; as it was Presented at Court.   1616.
>> Head-title only.
>> A Masque Presented in the House of the Right Honorable the Lord Haye. . . . On Saturday the 22. of February, 1617.
>> This has a separate titlepage without imprint, but dated 1617.   It was entitled *Lovers made Men* in the separate edition of that date, while Gifford named it the *Masque of Lethe*.
>> The Vision of Delight Presented at Court in Christmas, 1617.
>> Pleasure reconciled to Virtue.   A Masque.   As it was Presented at Court before King Iames.   1619.
>> For the Honour of Wales.

Newes from the new World Discover'd in the Moone. A Masque, as it was Presented at Court before King Iames. 1620.
These have head-titles only.

A Masque of the Metamorphos'd Gypsies. As it was thrice Presented to King Iames. First, at Burleigh on the Hill. Next, at Belvoyr. And lastly, at Windsor. August, 1621.
With separate title page without imprint.

The Masque of Augures. With the several Antimasques Presented on Twelfe-night, 1622.

Time Vindicated to himselfe, and to his Honors. In the presentation at Court on Twelfth night. 1623.

Neptunes Triumph for the Returne of Albion. Celebrated in a Masque At the Court on the Twelfth night. 1624.

Pans Anniversarie ; or, the Shepherds Holy-day . . . As it was presented at Court before King James. 1625.

The Masque of Owles at Kenelworth . . . . 1626.

The Fortunate Isles, and their Vnion. Celebrated in a Masque Design'd for the Court, on the Twelfth night. 1626.

Loves Triumph through Callipolis. Performed in a Masque at Court. 1630.

Chloridia. Rites to Chloris and her Nymphs. Personated in a Masque at Court. . . . At Shrove-tide. 1630.

These have head titles only.

At sig 2N4 (third register) in the section entitled *Underwood*, we further find, with head titles only :

The Kings Entertainment at Welbeck in Nottingham-shire, A house of the Right Honourable, William Earle of Newcastle, ... &c. At his going into Scotland. 1633.
[*Love's Welcome at Welbeck.*]

Loves Wel-come. The King and Queenes Entertainment at Bolsover : at The Earle of Newcastles, The thirtieth of Iuly, 1634.
[*Love's Welcome at Bolsover.*]

The Works of Ben Jonson . . . . MDCXCII.

See *Plays*, p. 56. Contains, at sig. 2Q4ᵛ and following, the masques as in folio 1640, vol. I; at sig. 4F the two masques from *Underwood* and at sig. 4G1ᵛ the other masques, as in folio 1640, vol. II, but with no separate titlepages.

B. Jon : his part of King James his Royall and Magnificent Entertainement through his Honorable Cittie of London, Thurseday the 15. of March. 1603. So much as was presented in the first and last of their Triumphall Arch's. With his speach made to the last Presentation, in the Strand, erected by the inhabitants of the Dutchy, and Westminster. Also, a briefe

Panegyre of his Maiesties first and well auspicated entrance to his high Court of Parliament, on Monday, the 19. of the same Moneth. With other Additions. *V. S. for Edward Blount,* 1604.

> Also contains with separate signatures, pagination and half-title, as follows :
>
>> A particular Entertainment of the Queene and Prince their Highnesse to Althrope, at the Right Honourable the Lord Spencers, on Saterday being the 25. of Iune 1603. as they came first into the Kingdome ; being written by the same Author, and not before published.
>
> B.M. (C. 39. d. 1.) Bodl. U.L.C. (impf.) T.C.C.

Q. Horatius Flaccus : His Art of Poetry. Englished by Ben: Jonson. With other Workes of the Author, never Printed before. *J. Okes, for John Benson.* 1640. 12mo.

> With engraved title signed W. M., containing bust, facing titlepage. Of this there are two states, distinguished by the imprint, one reading *for Iohn Benson,* the other *for Iohn Benson sold by W. Ley.* Among the undermentioned copies the short imprint is found in one of those in the Bodleian only.
>
> Among the "other Workes" is the *Masque of Gipsies* with separate title page on C 10.
>
> The Masque of the Gypsies. Written by Ben: Jonson. *J. Okes, for J. Benson,* 1640. Copies of both are in the Bodl.
>
> B.M. (1068. f. 7.) Bodl. (2 copies.) U.L.C. (impf.) Dyce.

The Characters of Two royall Masques. The one of Blacknesse, The other of Beautie. personated By the most magnificent of Queenes Anne Queene of great Britaine, &c. With her honorable Ladyes, 1605. and 1608. at White-hall : and Inuented by Ben: Ionson. *for Thomas Thorp.*

> Some copies (*e.g.* U.L.C. and Bodl.) read "White-Hall," the one letter alone apparently being altered. The Masque of Beauty begins with head-title at sig. C2^v.
>
> B.M. (C. 21. c. 56.) Bodl. U.L.C.

Hymenaei : or The Solemnities of Masque, and Barriers, Magnificently performed on the eleventh, [*sic*] and twelfth Nights, from Christmas ; At Court : To the auspicious celebrating of the Marriage-vnion, betweene Robert, Earle of Essex, and the Lady Frances, second Daughter to the most noble Earle of Suffolke. By Ben: Ionson. *Valentine Sims for Thomas Thorp.* 1606.

> B.M. (C. 34. d. 3.) Bodl.

The Masque of Queenes Celebrated From the House of Fame : By the most absolute in all State, And Titles. Anne Queene of Great Britaine, &c. With her Honourable Ladies. At White Hall, Febr. 2. 1609. Written by Ben: Ionson. *N. Okes for R. Bonian and H. Wally.* 1609.

> B.M. (C. 28. g. 5.). Bodl.

*Louers made Men. A Masque Presented in the House of the Right Honorable The Lord Haye. By diuers of noble qualitie, his friends. For the entertaynment of Monsieur le Baron de Tour, extraordinarie Ambassador for the French King. On Saterday the 22. of February. 1617. 1617.

> Bodl.

Loues Triumph through Callipolis. Performed in a Masque at Court 1630. By his Maiestie with the Lords, and Gentlemen assisting. The Inuentors. Ben. Ionson. Jnigo Iones. *I. N. for Thomas Walkley.* 1630.

> B.M. (644. b. 59.) Bodl.

The Masque of Augures. With the seuerall Antimasques. Presented on Twelfe night. 1621.

> The author's initials appear at the end.

> B.M. (C. 39. c. 34.). Bodl.

*Chloridia. Rites to Chloris and her Nymphs. Personated in a Masque, at Court. By the Queenes Maiesty And her ladies. At Shroue-tide. 1630. *for Thomas Walkley.*

> B.M. (C. 34. c. 58.) Bodl.

*The Fortunate Isles and their Vnion. celebrated in a Masque design'd for the Court, on the Twelfth night. 1624.

> B.M. (C. 33. e. 7. (4)). Bodl.

The Description of the Masque. With the Nuptiall Songs. Celebrating the happy Marriage of Iohn, Lord Ramsey, Viscount Hadington, with the Lady Elizabeth Ratcliffe, Daughter to the right Honor: Robert, Earle of Sussex. At Court On the Shroue-Tuesday at night. 1608. Deuised by Ben : Ionson.

> B.M. (C. 34. d. 4.) U.L.C. (impf.)

*Neptunes Triumph for the returne of Albion, celebrated in a Masque at the Court on the Twelfth night 1623.

> B.M. (644. b. 57. impf.) Bodl.

MIDDLETON, Thomas. (1570–1627.)

The Triumphs of Truth. A Solemnity vnparalleld for Cost, Art, and Magnificence, at the Confirmation and Establishment of that Worthy and true Nobly-minded Gentleman, Sir Thomas Middleton, Knight; in the Honorable Office of his Maiesties Lieuetenant, the Lord Maior of the thrice

Famous Citty of London.   Taking Beginning at his Lord-ships going, and
proceeding after his Returne from receiuing the Oath of Maioralty at Westminster, on the Morrow next after Simon and Iudes day, October 29. 1613.
All the Showes, Pageants, Chariots; Morning, Noone, and Night-Triumphes.
Directed, Written, and redeem'd into Forme, from the Ignorance of some
former times, and their Common Writer, By Thomas Middleton.   *Nicholas
Okes.*   1613.

> With the music at the end.
>
> B.M. (C. 33. e.)

[Re-issue.]   By Thomas Middleton.   Shewing also his Lordships Entertaine-
ment vpon Michaelmas day last, being the day of his Election, at that
most Famous and Admired Worke of the Running Streame, from Amwell-
Head into the Cesterne at Islington, being the sole Cost, Industry and
Inuention of the Worthy M^r. Hugh Middleton of London, Gold-smith.
Nicholas Okes.   1613.

> A re-issue of the sheets of the above with new title page and additional matter at
> the end, and with separate title-page as follows :
> The Manner of his Lordships Entertainment on Michaelmas day last, being the day
> of his Honorable Election, together with the worthy Sir Iohn Swinarton, Knight,
> then Lord Maior, the Learned and Iuditious, Sir Henry Montague, Maister
> Recorder, and many of the Right Worshipfull the Aldermen of the Citty of London.
> At that most Famous and Admired Worke of the Running Streame from Amwell
> Head, into the Cesterne neere Islington, being the sole Inuention, Cost, and
> Industry of that Worthy Maister Hugh Middleton, of London Goldsmith, for the
> generall good of the City.   By T. M.   *Nicholas Okes.*   1613.
>
> B.M. (C. 33. e.) Bodl.

Ciuitatis Amor.   The Cities Loue.   An entertainement by water, at Chelsey,
and White-hall.   At the ioyfull receiuing of that Illustrious Hope of Great
Britaine, the High and Mighty Charles, To bee created Prince of Wales,
Duke of Cornewall, Earle of Chester, &c.   Together with the Ample Order
and Solemnity of his Highnesse creation, as it was celebrated in his
Maiesties Palace of White-hall on Monday, the fourth of Nouember. 1616.
As also the Ceremonies of that Ancient and Honourable Order of the
Knights of the Bath ; And all the Triumphs showne in honour of his
Royall Creation.   *Nicholas Okes for Thomas Archer.* 1616.

> The author's name appears at the end of the " Entertainment," at sig. B2.
>
> B.M. (C. 33. d. 10.)

The Tryumphs of Honor and Industry.   A Solemnity performed through the
City, at the Confirmation and establishment of the Right Honorable,
George Bowles, In the Office of his Maiesties Lieuetenant, the Lord Mayor
of the famous City of London.   Taking beginning at his Lordships going,

and proceeding after his Returne from receiuing the Oath of Maioralty at Westminster, on the morrow next after Simon and Iudes day October 29. 1617. *Nicholas Okes.* 1617.

> The author's initials appear at the end of the epistle dedicatory.
>
> B.M. (11773. c. 6, titlepage mutilated.) Devon.

The Inner-Temple Masque. Or Masque of Heroes. Presented (as an Entertainement for many worthy Ladies :) By Gentlemen of the same Ancient and Noble House. Tho. Middleton. *for Iohn Browne.* 1619.

> B.M. (C. 34. d. 39.) Bodl.

The Triumphs of Loue and Antiquity. An Honourable Solemnitie performed through the Citie, at the confirmation and establishment of the Right Honourable Sir William Cockayn, Knight, in the office of his Maiesties Lieutenant, the Lord Maior of the Famous Citie of London : Taking beginning in the morning at his Lordships going, and perfecting it selfe after his returne from receiuing the oath of Maioralty at Westminster, on the morrow after Symon and Iudes Day, October 29. 1619. By Tho: Middleton. Gent. *Nicholas Okes.* 1619.

> B.M. (C. 34. d. 43.) Bodl.

A Courtly Masque : the Deuice Called The World tost at Tennis. As it hath beene diuers times Presented to the Contentment of many Noble and Worthy Spectators, By the Prince his Seruants. Inuented, and set downe, By Tho : Middleton & William Rowley Gent. *George Purslowe, sold by Edward Wright.* 1620.

> B.M. (11773. b. 6.) Bodl.

[Another issue] [Woodcut]. *George Purslowe, sold by Edward Wright.* 1620.

> The sheets of the above with the titlepage reset.
>
> B.M. (C. 34. d. 45. imprint cut.)

The Sunne in Aries. A noble Solemnity performed through the Citie, at the sole cost and charges of the Honourable and ancient Fraternity of Drapers, at at the confirmation and establishment of their most Worthy Brother the Right Honourable, Edward Barkham, in the high Office of his Maiesties Lieutenant, the Lord Maior of the famous Citie of London. Taking beginning at his Lordships going, and perfecting it selfe after his returne from receiuing the Oath of Maioralty at Westminster, on the morrow after Simon Iudes day, being the 29. of October. 1621. By Tho. Middleton. Gent. *Ed. All-de, for H. G.* 1621.

> B.M. (C. 33. e. 7. (18).)

Honorable Entertainments, Compos'de for the Seruice of this Noble Citie. Some of which were fashion'd for the Entertainment of the Lords of his Maiesties most Honorable Priuie Councell, vpon the Occasion of their late Royall Employment. Inuented by Thomas Middleton. *G. E.* 1621. 8vo.

> Haz. IV. 68. (Southeby's March 19. 1888. No. 114.)

The Triumphs of Honor and Virtue. A Noble Solemnity, performed through the City, at the sole Cost and Charges of the Honorable Fraternity of Grocers, at the Confirmation and Establishment of their most worthy Brother, the Right Honorable Peter Proby, in the high Office of his Majesty's Lieutenant, Lord Mayor and Chancellor of the famous City of London. Taking beginning at his Lordship's going, and perfecting it self after His return from receiving the Oath of Mayoralty at Westminster, on the Morrow after Simon and Judes Day, being the 29 of October, 1622. By Tho. Middleton, Gent. *Nicholas Okes.* 1622.

> Reprinted in the *Shakespeare Society Papers* (1845) from a copy in the possession of J. L. Pearson.
>
> B.M. (C. 33. e. 7. (13), wanting sig. A.)

The Triumphs of Integrity. A Noble Solemnity, performed through the City, at the sole Cost and Charges of the Honorable Fraternity of Drapers, at the Confirmation and Establishment of their most worthy Brother, the Right Honorable, Martyn Lumley, in the high Office of his Maiesties Lieutenant, Lord Maior and Chancellor of the famous City of London. Taking beginning at his Lordships going, and perfecting it selfe after His Returne from receiuing the Oath of Maioralty at Westminster, on the Morrow after Simon and Judes Day, being the 29. of October. 1623. By Tho. Middleton Gent. *Nicholas Okes.* 1623.

> Devon. (Haz. H. 394.)

The Triumphs of Health and Prosperity. A noble Solemnity performed through the City, at the sole Cost and Charges of the Honorable Fraternity of Drapers, at the Inauguration of their most Worthy Brother, The Right Honorable, Cuthbert Hacket, Lord Major of the Famous City of London. By Tho. Middleton Gent. [Woodcut.] *Nicholas Okes.* MDCXXVI.

> With a woodcut of the Drapers' arms on the titlepage.
>
> Guildhall Library.

MILTON, JOHN. (1608–1674.)

Poems of Mr. John Milton, both English and Latin, Compos'd at several times. Printed by his true Copies. The Songs were set in Musick by Mr. Henry Lawes Gentleman of the Kings Chappel, and one of His

Maiesties Private Musick. Printed and publish'd according to order. *Ruth Raworth for Humphrey Moseley.* 1645. 8vo.

> With an engraved portrait signed W. M. facing the titlepage.
> Contains *Arcades*, with head-title at sig. D2, and *Comus* with separate titlepage at E2:
>
> A Mask Of the same Author Presented At Ludlow-Castle, 1634. Before The Earl of Bridgewater, Then President of Wales. *Anno Dom.* 1645.
>
> B.M. (E. 1126. dated by Thomason "Jan: 2ᵈ.")

Poems, &c. upon Several Occasions. By Mr. John Milton: Both English and Latin, &c. Composed at several times. With a small Tractate of Education To Mr. Hartlib. *for Tho. Dring at the Blew Anchor.* 1673. 8vo.

> Contains *Arcades* and *Comus* with head titles at sigs. E3ᵛ & F2ᵛ.
>
> B.M. (1076. f. 19.) Bodl. U.L.C.

[Another issue.] *for Tho. Dring at the White Lion.* 1673. 8vo.

> The imprint alone differs.
>
> B.M. (684. d. 34.) Bodl.

The Poetical Works of Mr. John Milton. Containing, Paradise Lost, Paradise Regain'd, Sampson Agonistes, and his Poems on several Occasions. Together with Explanatory Notes on each Book of the Paradise Lost, and a Table never before Printed. *for Jacob Tonson,* M DC XC V. Fol.

> Five parts, each with separate signatures, pagination and titlepages, preceded by a general titlepage and engraved portrait by R. White. The fourth part has the following titlepage:—
>
> Poems upon Several Occasions. Compos'd at several times. By Mr. John Milton. The Third Edition. *for Jacob Tonson.* 1695.
>
> *Comus* and *Arcades* begin at sig. C1ᵛ and †D2ᵛ respectively. The B.M. copy is on L.P.
>
> B.M. (11,607. k. 5.) U.L.C.

---

*A Maske Presented At Ludlow Castle, 1634: On Michaelmasse night, before the Right Honorable, Iohn Earle of Bridgewater, Viscount Brackley, Lord Præsident of Wales, And one of His Maiesties most honorable Privie Counsell. *for Humphrey Robinson.* 1637.

> The dedication is signed by the composer, "H. Lawes."
>
> B.M. (C. 34. d. 46.) Bodl. T.C.C.

MUNDAY, ANTHONY. (1553–1633.)

Chruso-thriambos. The Triumphes of Golde. At the Inauguration of Sir Iames Pemberton, Knight, in the Dignity of Lord Maior of London : On Tuesday, the 29. of October. 1611. Performed in the harty loue, and at the charges of the Right Worshipfull, Worthy, and Ancient Company of Gold-Smithes. Deuised and Written by A. M. Cittizen and Draper of London. *William Iaggard.* 1611.

    T.C.C. Devon.

Himatia-Poleos. The Triumphs of olde Draperie, or the rich Cloathing of England. Performed in affection, and at the charges of the right Worthie and first honoured Companie of Drapers : at the enstalment of S^r. Thomas Hayes Knight, in the high office of Lord Maior of London, on Satturday, being the 29. day of October. 1614. Deuised and written by A. M. Citizen and Draper of London. *Edward Allde.* 1614.

    B.M. (C. 33. e. 7 (22).)

Metropolis Coronata, The Triumphes of Ancient Drapery : or, Rich Cloathing of England, in a second Yeeres performance. In Honour of the aduancement of Sir Iohn Iolles, Knight, to the high Office of Lord Maior of London, and taking his Oath for the same authoritie, on Monday, being the 30. day of October. 1615. Performed in heartie affection to him, and at the bountifull charges of his worthy Brethren the truely Honourable Society of Drapers, the first that receiued such Dignitie in this Citie. Deuised, and written, by A. M. Citizen, and Draper of London. *George Purslowe.* 1615.

    B.M. (C. 33. e. 7. (7).) Bodl.

Chrysanaleia : The Golden Fishing : Or, Honour of Fishmongers. Applauding the aduancement of M^r. Iohn Leman, Alderman, to the dignitie of Lord Maior of London. Taking his Oath in the same authority at Westminster, on Tuesday, being the 29. day of October. 1616. Performed in hearty loue to him, and at the charges of his worthy Brethren, the ancient, and right Worshipfull Company of Fishmongers. Deuised and written by A. M. Citizen and Draper of London. *George Purslowe.* 1616.

    The author's name appears in full at the end of the epistle dedicatory.

    B.M. (C. 33. e. 7. (14).) Bodl.

Sidero-Thriambos. Or Steele and Iron Triumphing. Applauding the aduancement of Sir Sebastian Haruey, Knight, to the dignitie of Lord Maior of London. Taking his oath in the same authoritie at Westminster, on Thursday, being the 29. day of October. 1618. Performed in hearty

loue to him, and at the charges of his kinde Brethren, the right Worshipfull
Company of Ironmongers. Deuised and written by A. M. Citizen and
Draper of London. *Nicholas Okes.* 1618. Partly 𝔅.𝔏.

> B.M. (C. 33. e. 7. (20).)

[Running title :] Camp-bell, or The Ironmongers Faire Field.

> The only known copy wants sig. A. It belongs to 1609.
> B.M. (C. 33. e. 7. (23). impf.)

The Triumphes of re-vnited Britania. Performed at the cost and charges of
the Right Worship: Company of the Merchant-Taylors, in honor of Sir
Leonard Holliday kni: to solemnize his entrance as Lorde Mayor of the
Citty of London, on Tuesday the 29. of October. 1605. Deuised and
Written by A. Mundy, Cittizen and Draper of London. *W. Jaggard.*

> B.M. (C. 33. e. 7 (3), impf.). Bodl.

NABBES, Thomas. (1605–1641 ?)

Plays, Masques, Epigrams, Elegies, and Epithalamiums . . . . . . 1639.

> See Addenda to *Plays*, p. cxxvii. The collection contains the separate issue of
> 1638, as below.

_____

The Springs Glorie. Vindicating Love by temperance against the tenent,
Sine Cerere & Baccho friget Venus. Moralized in a Maske. With other
Poems, Epigrams, Elegies, and Epithalamiums of the Authors Thomas
Nabbes. *I. D. for Charles Greene, sold by Nicolas Fussell.* 1638.

> Also contains, with head-title at sig. F1 :
> A Presentation Intended for the Prince his Highnesse on his Birth-day, the 29
> of May, 1638. annually celebrated.
> B.M. (C. 34. d. 49.) Bodl.

[Re-issue]. The Springs Glory, a Maske. Together With sundry Poems,
Epigrams, Elegies, and Epithalamiums. By Thomas Nabbs. *I. Dawson.*
1639.
> The sheets of the above re-issued with a new titlepage and dedication.
> B.M. (162. d. 45.) Bodl.

NELSON, Thomas. (*fl.* 1580.)

The Deuice of the Pageant: Set forth by the Worshipfull Companie of the
Fishmongers, for the right honourable Iohn Allot: established Lord Maior
of London, and Maior of the Staple for this present yeere of our Lord
1590. By T. Nelson. *London.* 1590. 𝔅.𝔏.

> B.M. (C. 38. d. 25.)

PEELE, George.   (1558 ?–1597 ?)

The Device of the Pageant borne before Woolstone Dixi Lord Maior of the
   Citie of London.   An. 1585.   October 29.   *Edward Allde.*   1585.
>   The author's name appears at the end.
>   Bodl.

Descensus Astrææ.   The Deuice of a Pageant, borne before M. William Web,
   Lord Maior of the Citie of London on the day he tooke his oath ; beeing
   the 29. of October. 1591.   Wherevnto is annexed A Speech deliuered by
   one clad like a Sea Nymph, who presented a Pinesse on the water brauely
   rigd and mand, to the Lord Maior, at the time he tooke Barge to go to
   Westminster.   Done by G. Peele Maister of Arts in Oxford.   *for William
   Wright.*
>   Guildhall Library.

RANDOLPH, Thomas.   (1605–1635.)

Poems . . . . . . 1652.
>   See *Plays*, p. 87.   This and all subsequent editions contain both *Aristippus* and
>   the *Conceited Pedlar.*

---

*Aristippus, Or The Iouiall Philosopher : Demonstratiuelie proouing, That
   Quartes, Pintes, and Pottles, Are sometimes necessary Authours in a
   Scholers Library.   Presented in a priuate Shew.   To which is added, The
   Conceited Pedlar.   *Thomas Harper, for Iohn Marriot, sold by Richard
   Mynne.*   M.DC.XXX.
>   The *Pedlar,* with head-title, begins at sig. E1.
>   Bodl.   U.L.C.   Dyce.

   *Aristippus, or The Iouiall Philosopher : Presented in a priuate Shew.
   To which is added, The Conceited Pedler.   *for Robert Allot,* MDCXXX.
>   The *Pedlar,* with head-title, begins at sig. E1.
>   B.M. (C. 34. e. 1.)

   *[Another edition.]   *for Robert Allot,* MDCXXXI.
>   The *Pedlar,* with head-title, begins at sig. E1.
>   B.M. (1346. b. 18.)   Bodl.

   *[Another edition.]   *for Robert Allot* MDCXXXV.
>   The *Pedlar,* with head-title, begins at sig. E1.
>   B.M. (644. c. 10.)   Bodl.   T.C.C.

*Aristippus Or The Ioviall Philosopher : Demonstrativelie prooving, That quartes, pointes, and Pottles. Are sometimes necessary Authors in a scholar's Library. Presented in a Private Shew. To which is added The Conceited Pedlar. *Dublin, Printed by the Society of Stationers, Printers to the Kings most Excellent Majesty.*

> The *Pedlar*, with head-title, begins at sig. D3.
>
> B.M. (12,316. d. 31., titlepage defective.)

SHIRLEY, JAMES. (1596–1666.)

Poems &c. By James Shirley. *for Humphrey Moseley.* 1646. 8vo.

> The volume consists of three parts, namely *Poems, Narcissus* and the *Triumph of Beauty*, each with separate titlepage (with similar imprint), pagination, and signatures. It appears, however, from Moseley's advertisement (see *Essay*, Apx. I. p. xxiv.) that they formed one publication, though the masque is sometimes found alone (*e.g.*, B.M. C. 12. f. 19 (1)). The volume has an engraved portrait by W. Marshall prefixed. The separate title to the Masque is as follows :
>
> The Triumph of Beautie. As it was personated by some young Gentlemen for whom it was intended at a private Recreation. By James Shirley. *for Humphrey Moseley.* MDCXLVI.
>
> B.M. (1076. f. 8.) Bodl. T.C.C.

Honoria and Mammon. . . . . . . 1659. 8vo.

> See *Plays*, p. 110. The signatures and pagination to both parts are continuous. The separate titlepage to the second at sig. İi1, runs as follows :—
>
> The Contention of Ajax and Ulysses, for the Armor of Achilles. As it was nobly represented by young Gentlemen of quality, at a private Entertainment of some persons of Honour. Written By James Shirley. *for John Crook.*

A Contention for Honour and Riches. By J. S. *E. A. for William Cooke.* 1633.

> The author's name appears in full at the end of the epistle dedicatory.
> An altered and enlarged edition appeared under the title *Honoria and Mammon.* See *Plays*, p. 110.
>
> B.M. (C. 12. f. 15 (5)). Bodl.

The Triumph of Peace. A Masque, presented by the Foure Honourable Houses, or Jnnes of Court. Before the King and Queenes Majesties, in the Banquetting-house at White Hall, February the third, 1633. Invented and Written, By James Shirley, of Grayes Inne, Gent. *Iohn Norton, for William Cooke.* 1633.

> Sig. A1ᵛ, l. 19, reads "bride" by misprint for "bridle."
>
> B.M. (644. c. 44.) Bodl.

[Another issue.]   *Iohn Norton, for William Cooke.*   1633.

> Same titlepage as above but text corrected throughout and largely reset.   Sig. A1ᵛ,
> l. 19, reads "bridle," correctly.
>
> > B.M. (C. 12. f. 15 (7)).   Bodl.   U.L.C.   Dyce.

[Another issue.]   The third Impression.   *Iohn Norton, for William Cooke.*   1633.

> The corrected sheets issued with the alteration on the titlepage.
>
> > Dyce.

[Another issue.]   By Iames Shirley, Gent.   *Iohn Norton, for William Cooke.*   1633.

> The corrected sheets issued with a different title page.
>
> > Bodl.

Cupid and Death.   A Masque.   As it was Presented before his Excellencie The Embassadour of Portugal, Upon the 26. of March, 1653.   Written by J.S.   *T. W. for J. Crook & J. Baker,* 1653.

> > B.M. (644 c. 64.)

Cupid and Death.   A Private Entertainment, represented with scenes & musick, vocall & instrumentall.   Writen by J. S.   *for John Crooke and John Playford.* 1659.

> > B.M. (644. c. 66.)   Bodl.

SIDNEY, Sir Philip.   (1554–1586.)

The Countesse of Pembrokes Arcadia.   Written by Sir Philip Sidney Knight. Now the third time published, with sundry new additions of the same Author.   *for William Ponsonbie.*   1598.   Fol.

> > Contains the *Entertainment of her Majesty at Wanstead* or the *Lady of May* with head-title at 3B3ᵛ.
> >
> > > B.M. (C. 40. k. 5.)

[Other editions.]

> > Subsequent editions containing the *Lady of May* appeared in 1599, 1605, 1613, 1621, 1623, 1627, 1629, 1633, 1638, 1655, 1662, and 1674, details of which will be found in Dr. Sommer's edition.   To these may be added that of 1622 (Haz. II. 559) which alone is not to be found in the B.M.

SQUIRE, John.   (*fl.* 1620.)

Tes Irenes Trophæa.   Or, the Tryumphs of Peace.   That Celebrated the Solemnity of the right Honourable Sʳ Francis Iones Knight, at his Inauguration into the Maioraltie of London, on Monday being the 30

of October, 1620. At the particular cost and charge of the right
worshipfull and ancient Society of the Haberdashers. With explication of
the seuerall shewes and deuices by I. S. *Nicholas Okes*, 1620.

> The author's name appears in full at the end of the epistle dedicatory. With the
> music.
> Guildhall Library.

TAYLOR, JOHN. (1580–1653.)

The Triumphs of Fame and Honour: at the Inauguration of Robert
Parkhurst, Cloth-worker, Compiled by John Taylor, the Water-Poet. 1634.

> Haz. H. 599.

TOWNSEND, AURELIAN. (*fl.* 1601–1643.)

Albions Triumph. Personated in a Maske at Court. By the Kings Maiestie
and his Lords. The Sunday after Twelfe Night. 1631. *Aug : Mathewes
for Robert Allet.* 1631.

> The author's name appears at the end : " Aurelian Tounshend."
> B.M. (162. e. 16.)

*[Another issue.] *Aug : Mathewes for Robert Allet.* 1631.

> Identical with the above, except for the omission of the author's name.
> B.M. (644. c. 81.) Bodl.

Tempe Restord. A Masque Presented by the Queene, and foureteene Ladies,
to the Kings Maiestie at Whitehall on Shrove-Tuesday. 1631. *A. M. for
Robert Allet and George Bakek.* [sic.] 1631.

> On the recto of the last leaf (p. 19) occurs the statement, " All the Verses were
> written by Mr. Aurelian Townesend."
> B.M. (644. c. 82.) Bodl.

WEBSTER, JOHN. (1580?–1625?)

Monuments of Honor. Deriued from remarkable Antiquity and Celebrated
in the Honorable City of London, at the sole Munificent charge and
expences of the Right Worthy and Worshipfull Fraternity of the Eminent
Merchant Taylors. Directed in their most affectionate Loue at the
Confirmation of their right Worthy Brother Iohn Gore in the High Office
of His Maiesties Lieutenant over this Royall Chamber. Expressing in a
Magnificent Tryumph, all the Pageants, Chariots of Glory, Temples of
Honor, besides a specious and goodly Sea Tryumph, as well particularly to
the Honor of the City, as generally to the Glory of this our Kingdome.
Invented and written by Iohn Webster Merchant-Taylor. *Nicholas Okes.*
1624. 4to.

> Devon.

AUTHORS UNKNOWN.

All editions are anon. unless otherwise stated.

The Speeches and Honorable Entertainment giuen to the Queenes Maiestie in Progresse, at Cowdrey in Sussex, by the right Honorable the Lord Montacute. 1591. *Thomas Scarlet, solde by William Wright.* 1591.

> B.M. (C. 33. d. 11.)

The Honorable Entertainement gieuen to the Queenes Maiestie in Progresse, at Eluetham in Hampshire, by the right Honorable the Earle of Hertford. 1591 *Iohn Wolfe.* 1591.

> Contains a folding plate.

> B.M. (C. 33. e. 7. (9), impf.)   U.L.C.

> [Another edition.]   Newly corrected and amended.   1591.

> Haz. H. 182.

Speeches deliuered to her Maiestie this last progresse, at the Right Honorable the Lady Russels, at Bissam, the Right Honorable the Lorde Chandos at Sudley, at the Right Honorable the Lord Norris, at Ricorte. *Oxforde, Joseph Barnes.* 1592.

> B.M. (C. 33. e. 7 (19).   Impf., titlepage in facs.)

Ane verie excellent and delectabill Treatise intitulit Philotus. Quhairin we may persaue the greit inconveniences [*sic*] that fallis out in the Mariage betwene age and zouth. *Edinburgh, Robert Charteris.* 1609. *Cum priuilegio regali.* 𝕭.𝕷.

> With the Scottish Arms on recto of leaf preceding titlepage.

> B.M. (C. 34. b. 39.)

> A verie excellent and delectable Comedie, Intituled Philotus. Wherein we may perceiue the great inconveniences [*sic*] that fall out in the mariage betweene olde age and youth. *Edinburgh, Andro Hart.* 1612. 𝕭.𝕷.

> B.M. (C. 34. b. 40.)

Londons Loue, to the royal Prince Henrie, meeting him on the Riuer of Thames, at his returne from Richmonde, with a worthie fleete of her Cittizens, on Thursday the last of May, 1610. With a breife reporte of the water Fight, and Fire workes. *Edw. Allde, for Nathaniell Fosbrooke,* 1610.

> With woodcuts on recto and verso of leaf preceding titlepage.

> B.M. (C. 33. d. 5.)

The Maske of Flowers. Presented By the Gentlemen of Graies-Inne, at the Court of White-hall, in the Banquetting House, vpon Twelfe night, 1613. Being the last of the Solemnities and Magnificences which were performed at the marriage of the right honourable the Earle of Somerset, and the Lady Francis daughter of the Earle of Suffolke, Lord Chamberlaine. *N. O. for Robert Wilson.* 1614.

> The epistle dedicatory to Sir Francis Bacon is signed I.G., W.D., and T.B. With the music at the end.
>
> B.M. (C. 34. b. 33.) Bodl.

A merrie Dialogue, Betwene Band, Cuffe, and Ruffe : Done by an excellent Wit, And Lately acted in a shew in the famous Vniversitie [*sic*] of Cambridge. *William Stansby for Miles Partrich.* 1615.

> B.M. (12,315. h. 50.)

Exchange Ware at the second hand, Viz. Band, Ruffe, and Cuffe, lately out, and now newly dearned vp. Or Dialogue, acted in a Shew in the famous Vniuersitie of Cambridge. The second Edition. *W. Stansby for Myles Partrich.* 1615.

> B.M. (C. 34. b. 5.)

A Merry Dialogue between Band, Cuff, and Ruff. Done by an excellent Wit. And Lately acted in a Shew in the famous Vniversity of Cambridge. *for F. K.,* 1661.

> B.M. (643. c. 3.)

Worke for Cutlers. Or, a merry Dialogue betweene Sword, Rapier, and Dagger. Acted in a Show in the famous vniuersitie of Cambridge. *Thomas Creede, for Richard Meighen and Thomas Iones.* 1615.

> B.M. (1076. i. 15.)

Wine, Beere, and Ale, together by the Eares. A Dialogue, Written first in Dutch by Gallobelgicus, and faithfully translated out of the originall Copie, by Mercurius Brittanicus, for the benefite of his Nation. *A. M. for Iohn Groue.* 1629.

> B.M. (162. e. 27.)

Wine, Beere, Ale, and Tobacco. Contending for Superiority. A Dialogue. The second Edition, much enlarged. *T. C. for Iohn Groue,* 1630.

> B.M. (643. c. 62.) Bodl.

[Another edition.]   A Dialogue.   *J. B. for John Groue*, 1658.
    With woodcut facing titlepage.
        B.M. (643. c. 63.)

The Entertainment of the High and Mighty Monarch Charles King of Great
    Britaine, France, and Ireland, Into his auncient and royall City of
    Edinburgh, the fifteenth of Iune, 1633.   *Edinburgh by Iohn Wreittoun.*
    1633.
        B.M. (C. 34. b. 11.)   U.L.C.

Corona Minervæ.   Or a Masque Presented before Prince Charles his High-
    nesse, The Duke of Yorke his Brother, and the Lady Mary his Sister, the
    27th of February, at the Colledge of the Museum Minervæ.   *for William
    Sheares.*   1635.
        B.M. (C. 40. c. 19 (2)).   Bodl.

The King and Queenes Entertainement at Richmond.   After their departure
    from Oxford: In a Masque, presented by the most Illustrious Prince,
    Prince Charles, Sept. 12. 1636.   *Oxford. Leonard Lichfield*, M.DC.XXXVI.
        B.M. (C. 33. d. 8.)   Bodl.

Luminalia, or The Festivall of Light.   Personated in a Masque at Court, By
    the Queenes Majestie, and her Ladies.   On Shrovetuesday Night, 1637.
    Iohn Haviland for Thomas Walkley, 1637.
        B.M. (643. c. 29.)   Bodl.

A new Play Called Canterburie His Change of Diot.   Which sheweth
    variety of wit and mirth: privately acted neare the Palace-yard at
    Westminster.   In th' 1 Act, the Bishop of Canterbury having variety of
    dainties, is not satisfied till he be fed with tippets of mens eares.   2 Act,
    he hath his nose held to the Grinde-stone.   3 Act, he is put into a bird
    Cage with the Confessor.   4 Act, The Jester tells the King the Story.
    Printed Anno Domini, 1641.
        B.M. (E. 177. (8).)   T.C.C. (impf.)

Gesta Grayorum: or, the History Of the High and mighty Prince, Henry
    Prince of Purpoole, Arch-Duke of Stapulia and Bernardia, Duke of High
    and Nether Holborn, Marquis of St. Giles and Tottenham, Count Palatine
    of Bloomsbury and Clerkenwell, Great Lord of the Cantons of Islington,
    Kentish-Town, Paddington and Knights-bridge, Knight of the most

Heroical Order of the Helmet, and Sovereign of the Same. Who Reigned and Died, A.D. 1594. Together with A Masque, as it was presented (by His Highness's Command) for the Entertainment of Q. Elizabeth; who, with the Nobles of both Courts, was present thereat. *for W. Canning,* MDCLXXXVIII. Price one shilling.

> The first part only.
> B.M. (643. d. 30.)

ADDENDA.

BEAUMONT and FLETCHER. To the collected editions add :

Poems: by Francis Beaumont, Gent. Viz. The Hermaphrodite. The Remedy of Love. Elegies. Sonnets, with other Poems. *for Laurence Blaiklock.* 1653. 8vo.

> The masque is found, with head-title at sig. G6.
> B.M. (E. 1236, dated by Thomason: Febr. 10. 1652.)

[Another issue.] *for William Hope.* 1653. 8vo.

> The sheets of the above re-issued with a new titlepage.
> B.M. (E. 1455, dated by Thomason: Nou. 22.)

Poems. The golden remains of those so much admired dramatick poets, Francis Beaumont & John Fletcher, Gent. Containing The hermaphrodite two sexes. The remedy and art of love. Elegies on the most eminent persons; with other amorous sonnets, and conceited fancies. Together with the prologues epilogues and songs, many of which were never before inserted in his printed playes. The second edition enriched with the addition of other drolleries by several wits of these present times. *for William Hope.* 1660. 8vo.

> The sheets of the above again re-issued with a new titlepage.
> (Potter's Bibl. of B. and F.)

I.—INDEX OF AUTHORS.

II.—INDEX OF TITLES.

N.B.—Masques, etc., having no title in the old copies are indexed under the place of representation. Modern titles are enclosed in brackets.

Althrope, Entertainment of the Queen and Prince at. Jonson, Ben. (1604.)
Amphrissa. Heywood, Thomas.
Apollo and Daphne. Heywood, Thomas.
Arcades. Milton, John.
Aristippus. Randolph, Thomas. 1630.
Albion's Triumph. Townsend, Aurelian. 1631.
Augurs, The Masque of. Jonson, Ben. n.d.

Band, Cuff and Ruff. Author unknown. 1615.
Beauty, The Masque of. Jonson, Ben. (n.d.)
Beauty, The Triumph of. Shirley, James. (1646.)
Bissam, Speeches to her Majesty at. Author unknown. 1592.
Blackness, The Masque of. Jonson, Ben. (n.d.)
Bretbie, Masque at. Cockayne, Sir Aston.
Britannia Triumphans. D'avenant, Sir William. 1637.
Britannia's Honour. Dekker, Thomas. 1628.

Campbell. Munday, Anthony. n.d.
Canterbury his Change of Diet. Author unknown. 1641.
Cawsome House, Entertainment at. Campion, Thomas. 1613.
Challenge at Tilt, A. Jonson, Ben. (1616.)
Chester's Triumph. Amerie, Robert. 1610.
Chloridia. Jonson, Ben. n.d.
Christmas his Masque. Jonson, Ben. (1640.)
Chruso-thriambos. Munday, Anthony. 1611.
Chrysanaleia. Munday, Anthony. 1616.
Civitas Amor. Middleton, Thomas. 1616.
Coelum Britannicum. Carew, Thomas. 1634.
Comus. *See* Ludlow Castle, Masque at.
Conceited Pedlar, The. Randolph, Thomas. 1630.

Contention for Honour and Riches, A. Shirley, James. 1633.
Contention of Ajax and Ulysses, The. Shirley, James. (1659.)
Cornwallis, Sir William, his house at Highgate, Entertainment of the King and Queen at. Jonson, Ben. (1616.)
Corona Minervae. Author unknown. 1635.
Cowdrey, Speeches and Entertainment of the Queen at. Author unknown. 1591.
Cruelty of the Spaniards in Peru, The. D'avenant, Sir William. 1658.
Cupid and Death. Shirley, James. 1653.

Death, The Triumph of. See *Plays*, Four Plays in One.
Descensus Astrææ. Peele, George. n.d.
Dixie, Woolstone, Pageant before. Peele, George. 1585.
Drake, The History of Sir Francis. D'avenant, Sir William. 1659.

Edinburgh, Entertainment of King Charles into. Author unknown. 1633.
Elizabeth, Queen, and the French Ambassadors, The Shews, etc., before. Goldwell, Henry. n.d.
Elvetham, Entertainment to the Queen at. Author unknown. 1591.
Exchange Ware at Second Hand. Author unknown. Band, Cuff and Ruff. 1615 (1615).

Fame and Honour, The Triumph of. Taylor, John. 1634.
Flowers, The Masque of. Author unknown. 1614.
For the Honour of Wales. Jonson, Ben. (1640.)

D

ESSAY INTRODUCTORY.

ESSAY INTRODUCTORY. *

THE present essay may serve as at once an introduction and an appendix to the *List of English Plays* issued by the Society in 1900; an introduction in so far as it deals with my predecessors in the field of dramatic bibliography, an appendix in so far as it seeks to throw light on some of the puzzles which the ingenuity and carelessness of seventeenth century printers and stationers have bequeathed to a curious posterity.

The earliest lists of printed plays, as distinct from those of plays licensed or acted, are to be found in the advertisements of published or forthcoming works which stationers in the seventeenth century, as now, were in the habit of appending to their publications. A fair number of these are extant, though so far none has been found earlier than 1649, and the contents are often interesting both as affording information concerning editions no longer extant and as throwing light on the complicated business relations of individual stationers.† In the meantime, however, play-collecting had begun, and a sort of enterprising publishers started a second-hand trade in them. The exact date at which the fashion came in, cannot, of course, be fixed with accuracy, but in 1671 Francis Kirkman, the publisher, wrote " I have been these twenty years a Collector of them, and have conversed with, and enquired of those that have been collecting these fifty years," which would carry it back to about 1620. The catalogue of an early collection belonging, apparently, to a Henry Oxenden, of Barham, is preserved in a manuscript in the possession of Mr. A. H. Huth, the entries in which range from 1647 to 1660. The earliest

---

* The substance of this essay has been already made public to the Society in a paper read at the February Meeting, 1901.

† Specimen lists, with notes on these points, will be found in Appendix I.

E

suggestion of a second-hand trade, however, is contained in an edition of Goffe's *Careless Shepherdess*, published by Richard Rogers and William Ley in 1656, which contains "an exact and perfect Catalogue of all Plays that are Printed," for though it is not definitely stated that the plays are offered for sale, it is probable that the catalogue was compiled with that intention. The pretensions of the list from the bibliographical point of view are of a primitive character; it is merely an alphabetical list of titles, with an occasional mention of the author's name, and its claims to accuracy are equally slight. Thus, among other astonishing entries, we find plays on *Edward II, III,* and *IV* all ascribed to Shakespeare, and the *Revenge of Bussy* to a person of the name of 'Damboise,' while John Cooke's play, *Greene's Tu Quque* appears as *Greens tu quoque cookt !* Nevertheless, grotesquely inaccurate as this and the subsequent stationers' lists are, they are in many cases of the highest importance, both as preserving record of plays now no longer to be found, and as occasionally throwing a useful, if in no case very trustworthy, light on points of authorship.*

Later in the same year, 1656,† another stationer, Edward Archer, dwelling at the sign of the Adam and Eve in Little Britain, issued a play by Massinger, Middleton and Rowley, entitled the *Old Law*, to which he appended "an exact and perfect Catalogue of all the Playes, with the Authors Names . . . . more exactly Printed then ever before," all of which "you may either have at the Signe of the Adam and Eve, in Little

---

* For these reasons it has been thought worth while to reprint the lists *in extenso* with notes. *See* Appendix II.

† The imprint bears the date 1656, but in the copy in the British Museum this has been altered in a contemporary hand to Aug. 6. 1655. If this date were correct, it would almost necessarily place the list before that of Rogers and Ley, but there are good reasons to suppose that it is a mistake. In the first place, the entry on the title page (*see* Apx. II.) implies the existence of a former list, and none but that appended to the *Careless Shepherdess* is known; secondly, the more elaborate character of the present list, as well as many minute points of internal evidence, combine to place it later, and lastly, although the practice of post-dating was extremely common then as now (witness the valuable entries made by Thomason in the tracts he collected), it is next to impossible to suppose that book should have been published bearing a date more than seven months ahead,

Britain; or, at the Ben Jonson's Head in Thredneedle-street, over against the Exchange." The latter was the shop belonging to another stationer, Robert Pollard. This list, though making greater bibliographical pretensions than its predecessor, contains blunders no less startling The supposed author's name is in most cases added, as also letters, C, T, H, I, M, P, indicating the nature of the piece (*i.e.*, comedy, tragedy, history, interlude, masque, or pastoral). The compiler appears to have had little knowledge of the subject beyond what could be gathered from the titlepages themselves, and he sometimes omits the author's name in cases where it must have been matter of common knowledge. The list runs to some 600 items, or about a hundred more than its predecessor, and like it contains a certain number of titles that have not been identified. The amount of authority to be attached to the entries may be gathered from the fact that *Phillis of Scyros* appears as *Scirio and Phillis*, that *Arden of Faversham* is attributed to Richard Bernard, *Love's Labour's Lost* to Will. Sampson, and the *Trick to Catch the Old One* to Will. Shakespeare.

By far the best known and most important, however, of the early play-collectors and vendors was Francis Kirkman, who started in the bookselling trade immediately after the Restoration, and has left interesting references to his business ventures in the prefaces to some of his editions. Among his first publications was *A Cure for a Cuckold*, which issued from the press in 1661, and which he ascribed to Webster and Rowley.* Prefixed is an address headed "The Stationer, to the Judicious Reader," in which he writes : " It was not long since I was only a Book-Reader, and not a Book-seller, which Quality (my former Employment somewhat failing, and I being unwilling to be idle) I have now lately taken on me. It hath been my fancy and delight (ere since I knew any thing) to converse with Books ; and the pleasure I have taken in those of this nature, (viz. *Plays*) hath bin so extraordinary, that it hath bin much to my cost; for I have been (as we term it) a Gatherer of *Plays* for some years, and I am confident I have

---

* As early as 1657 *Lust's Dominion* appeared, printed "for F.R.," with an epistle dedicatory signed by Kirkman, but he probably merely financed the publishing of the piece, which was " to be sold by Robert Pollard."

more of several sorts than any man in *England*, Book-seller, or other;
I can at any time shew 700 in number, which is within a small matter
all that were ever printed. Many of these I have several times over, and
intend, as I sell, to purchase more ; All, or any of which, I shall be ready
either to sell or lend to you upon reasonable Considerations." He goes on
to promise for the same " Tearm " two other plays, to wit, *The Thracian
Wonder* and *Gammer Gurton's Needle*, of both of which editions are extant
dated 1661. In the preface to the *Thracian Wonder* he further says:
" I have several *Manuscripts* of this nature, written by worthy authors, and
I account it much pity they should now lye dormant, and buried in
oblivion, since ingenuity is so likely to be encouraged, by reason of the
happy Restauration of our Liberties. We have had the private Stage for
some years clouded, and under a tyrannical command, though the publick
Stage of *England* has produc'd many monstrous villains, some of which
have deservedly made their *exit*." It was, of course, a time of clover for
pedlars with such wares as Kirkman's for sale, and it may well be that his
second-hand book-trade was brisk ; he does not, however, seem to have
received any great encouragement in his attempts to revive old plays.
Besides those above-mentioned, he issued in the following year, 1662, and
in conjunction with Henry Marsh, Middleton's comedy, *Anything for a
Quiet Life*, and also the *Birth of Merlin*, ascribed on the titlepage to
Shakespeare and Rowley. In each case the play seems to have been
printed from a manuscript, which was definitely stated to be the case with
the *Cure for a Cuckold* and the *Thracian Wonder*. We have also a reprint
of Middleton and Rowley's *Spanish Gipsy* dated 1661,* published by
him, and one of the same year of the anonymous comedy of *The Two
Merry Milkmaids*, on the titlepage of which his name appears, together
with those of Brook, Johnson and Marsh. To 1661 also, and
to the same combination of booksellers, belongs the edition of
the *Tom Tyler*, to which was appended the first of Kirkman's

---

* Part of this edition, however, was published by R. Croft, and bears his name on
the titlepage.

lists of plays. His enterprises in the pre-Restoration drama are thus confined to the first two years of his business life, unless we count Sir Aston Cokayne's works, which he took over from Philemon Stephens the younger in 1662, and of which he put forth a new issue, differing however in titlepage only, in 1669. His desistance may have been due to the violent trade opposition he encountered in certain quarters, in which he seems to have been regarded in the light of an interloper. We get a hint of the bitterness of commercial jealousy among the publishers of the time, as well as the singular directness with which they acted on its promptings, in the titlepage of a play of Beaumont and Fletcher's published by a well known firm, or rather combination, which had been for half a generation successfully catering for the popular taste. It runs thus : " The Beggars Bush. Written by Francis Beaumont, And John Fletcher. Gentlemen. You may speedily expect those other Playes, which Kirkman, and his Hawkers have deceived the buyers withall, selling them at treble the value, that this and the rest will be Sold for, which are the Onely Originall and corrected copies, As they were first purchased by us at no mean rate, and since printed by us. London, Printed for Humphrey Robinson, and Anne Moseley, at the three Pigeons, and at the Princes Arms in Saint Pauls Church-yard, 1661." If we attach credence to these remarks we shall have to suppose that Kirkman was selling his plays at eighteen pence each, which is not very likely; moreover, his competition appears to have been perfectly legitimate, since I have failed to discover any case in which he pirated Moseley's editions, or in which their editions clashed.

At this time we find Kirkman dwelling at the John Fletcher's Head " on the back-side of St. Clements," while Henry Marsh, his partner in several of the above-mentioned enterprises, carried on business at the Prince's Arms in Chancery Lane, near Fleet street.* Other joint ventures of theirs were *Bottom the Weaver*, a farce or droll drawn from the *Midsummer Night's*

---

* Not to be confused with Humphrey Moseley's shop at the sign of the Prince's Arms in Paul's Churchyard, 1627–1660 (Anne Moseley till 1664).

Dream, which appeared in 1661, and R. Nevile's *Poor Scholar,* which appeared the following year. After this we lose sight of Kirkman for a while. What he was doing in the interval between 1662 and 1666 it is impossible to say for certain, but it may be plausibly conjectured that not finding his capital sufficient to tide him over the earlier years of business, or for other reasons, he entered Marsh's establishment, possibly as a junior partner, though his name never appears as such on titlepages. In any case, when Marsh either died or retired from business in 1665, Kirkman certainly took over the copyrights and no doubt the stock also, as is evident from the fact that the later editions of Richard Head's very popular *English Rogue,* bear his imprint, whereas the earlier ones bear that of Henry Marsh. Moreover, he actually carried on his business at Marsh's shop, the Prince's Arms, in Chancery Lane, as appears from the imprints to the editions of C. Mollery's *Holland's Ingratitude* and of the *English Rogue,* published in 1666. For some years he seems mainly to have existed for and by publishing this latter work, numerous editions of the four parts of which range from 1666 to 1680. He occasionally, however, varied this stock dish by dramatic publications such as Jordan's *Money is an Ass* (1668), and Dancer's translation of Corneille's *Nicomede,* containing his second catalogue (1671), various editions of the famous collection of drolls entitled the *Wits,* and even an occasional and ill-assorting religious tract such as the *Course of Catechizing* of 1674. He did not, however, continue at the shop in Chancey Lane for long. In 1669 he was living "under St. Ethelborough's Church in Bishopsgate street" whence the *Psittacorum Regio* of that year was issued, while two years later we find him "in Thames-street over against the Custom-House," witness the *English Rogue* (Part II) of 1671 and the *Nicomede.* Lastly, in 1674, we find him issuing his own translation of the *History of Prince Erastus* from "his Shop in Fan-Church Street over against the Sign of the Robin Hood near Aldgate." The latest book bearing his name appeared in 1680, but this is only a reprint of the *English Rogue,* the last new publication which he issued being Whitcombe's *Janua Divorum* in 1678.

Thus Kirkman's dramatic catalogues appeared, with an interval of ten years between them, in 1661 when he first started in the trade, and in 1671 when, after some vicissitudes apparently, he had built up for himself or had inherited a certain publishing connection. In an interesting "Advertisement" added in 1671* he states that his first list contained 690 plays, his second 806. The difference is due to some hundred plays published during the interval and to the correction of certain omissions. The lists of course include Masques and similar pieces, an addition which is responsible for his statement that Jonson wrote fifty plays. He also states that he had himself seen all the plays he mentions "within ten" and possessed them all "within thirty." He gives in each case the author's name where known, the title of the play, and letters to indicate its nature. These latter are the same as in Archer's catalogue with the addition of TC for tragi-comedy. The list cannot lay claim to any very high authority—Kirkman's falling into the trap of ascribing *Selimus* to Goffe, should alone put that out of the question†—hardly perhaps to as much as, thanks chiefly to Langbaine, has commonly been attributed to it, but it is on the whole a careful compilation of a very different nature from its predecessors.

I need not here do more than mention Edward Phillips' *Theatrum Poetarum* of 1675, William Winstanley's *Lives of the most famous English Poets*, published in 1687, and Gerard Langbaine's *Account of the English Dramatic Poets*‡ which appeared in its final form in 1691, since the first is too superficial and the last too well known to call for comment, while the second may be said largely to combine both disqualifications. Nor need I say anything concerning later works of the same nature down to the opening of the nineteenth century, since a full and detailed list will be found at the end of the Introduction in the latest edition of Baker's

---

* *See* Appendix II, p. xliv.

† An error, by the way, in which he misled or was at least followed by Langbaine.

‡ Various copies containing MS. corrections and additions are in the British Museum, notably that annotated by Oldys, which has been largely used by subsequent writers on the subject.

Biographia Dramatica. That valuable work, first published by David Erskine Baker in 1764, was re-edited and continued by Isaac Reed in 1782, and again by Stephen Jones in 1812. It has come in for a good deal of abuse, and the third edition was severely criticised in the *Quarterly Review* by Octavius Gilchrist, to whom Jones replied in a pamphlet entitled "Hypercriticism Exposed."* The successive editors do not in any instance appear to have executed their work in a wholly satisfactory manner; still, the compilation compares not unfavourably with some subsequent work. †

The next attempt was made by Mr. Halliwell-Phillips in his *Dictionary of Old English Plays*, published in 1860, which is avowedly based on Langbaine and Baker, or more correctly on Baker and through him on Langbaine. A date-limit, however, of 1700 was fixed, and the whole of the biographical portion omitted, whereby, according to Mr. Fleay, it deprived itself of its chief recommendation to notice: Mr. Fleay shows himself, however, too utterly careless of accuracy in certain matters in which Mr. Halliwell is correct, for his opinion to carry much weight. Still, the bibliographical qualifications of the *Dictionary* are of a somewhat rudimentary character, and though from the point of view of dramatic history it was no doubt an advance on the *Biographia*, it cannot even in this respect be said to possess any very conspicuous merit.

In 1892 Mr. Halliwell-Phillips' *Dictionary* was somewhat enlarged on the same lines by Mr. W. C. Hazlitt in his *Manual for the Collector and Amateur of Old English Plays*. In spite of the fact that in many ways the work is the reverse of an improvement on its predecessor, Mr. Hazlitt

---

* This statement rests on the authority of Lowndes. It may, however, be mentioned that in a manuscript note in the British Museum copy the reply, which throughout speaks of Jones in the third person, is attributed to Gilchrist, while it might well on internal evidence be argued that the review was written by Gifford, who was editor at the time.

† That Stephen Jones might undoubtedly have made the book of very much greater value than he did would have been obvious enough even without the deserved, if somewhat brutal, thrashing he received at the hands of his reviewer, a thrashing his retort to which is equally piteous and pitiable, but the fact remains that his is absolutely the best edition of a work which has by no means as yet been altogether superseded.

saw fit to level at the author of the *Dictionary* not a little extravagant and patently absurd abuse. His right to throw stones may be gauged from the following lapses, amongst others, that adorn his own pages : the assertion that Jonson's *New Inn* was included, with the date 1631, "in the second volume" of his Works, whereas it first appeared in a collected edition in 1692 ; the inclusion of Day's *Peregrinatio*, which makes not the smallest pretence at being dramatic, while among the omissions are the political tract in dramatic form entitled *Canterbury his change of Diet*, and which is more important, Abraham Fraunce's translation of the *Aminta ;* the assertion that Chettle appears as part-author of *Sir John Oldcastle* in Henslowe's Diary ; and the ignorance in 1892 of the *Pilgrimage to Parnassus*, the manuscript of which had been recovered and published in 1886. In each of these cases, moreover, with the exception of course of the last, Mr. Hazlitt would have been saved from blundering had he implicitly followed the predecessor, who, he gives us to understand, had discharged his task in a manner incredibly negligent and perfunctory !

Lastly, and before quitting this part of my task, I may mention that the biographical side of the problem has been worked out with immense industry, though hardly, it must with regret be added, with equal judgment, by Mr. Fleay in his *Biographical Chronicle of the English Drama* which appeared in 1891. Since, however, he habitually sneers at and systematic- ally ignores the bibliographical side of the question, I do not feel called upon to make any detailed mention of his numerous misstatements.

It is, I presume, scarcely needful in an essay which will necessarily find such readers as fortune may afford it among the members of the Bibliographical Society, to seek in any way to vindicate the claims of the bibliographical study of our early drama. Such a study, moreover, is an essential preliminary to a satisfactory and scientific literary investigation. The fact that in my search for editions of old plays it was my good fortune to light on a perfect copy of the first edition of John Heywood's *Play of Love* only a few months after the piece had been edited from the imperfect and late Bodleian quarto, is a significant example of the use of the bibliographer in the field of literary criticism. It was, then, from this point of view that in 1897 I started making collections, of a purely bibliographical nature, in connection with our early dramatic literature, which led to the publication of the *List of English Plays,* and subsequently of the present volume by the Society.

To study the methods of dramatic publication in vogue in the seventeenth century is to a large extent to understand why the bibliography of the subject is at present in such an extraordinary state of confusion, since it is only after pursuing such a study for some time that the intricacy of many of the problems becomes apparent. In a sense it is true that such a delimitation as is implied in the term ' dramatic bibliography ' is essentially arbitrary, and that such a subject cannot properly be said to possess any unity; nevertheless, in practice, dramatic publications have for the most part, during the period under review, a certain character of their own, being highly popular pamphlets or books roughly, and often hurriedly, printed to meet an eager, but in most cases shortlived, demand, and issued at as low a price as possible, a price fixed by custom, at any rate during the earlier part of the period, at a ' tester '—sixpence. Such a volume as the 1616 folio of Ben Jonson is indeed a *rara avis* among dramatic publications of the time.

Piracy was of course rife, and though injunctions to stay publication seem at times to have been allowed, a stationer usually did very much as he pleased with any copy that happened to come into his hands. Something of this sort appears to have happened in the case of the 1609 quarto of *Troilus and Cressida.* In 1602–3 the piece was entered to Roberts conditionally upon his obtaining ' authority,' which he seems to have failed to do, since it was re-entered in 1608–9 to Bonian and Walley, who may, as Mr. Fleay suggests, have taken over the copy from Roberts on his leaving business in 1607. They published a quarto in the course of the year with the following seemingly authoritative titlepage: " The Historie of Troylus and Cresseïda. As it was acted by the Kings Maiesties seruants at the Globe. Written by William Shakespeare." To this, however, the

King's company appears to have taken exception, but the only result was the cancelling of the first leaf, which was replaced by a half-sheet containing a new titlepage and an enigmatically defiant preface, the later issue thus at first sight presenting the strange anomaly of a sheet of five leaves. The later titlepage ran : " The Famous History of Troylus and Cresseid. Excellently expressing the beginning of their loues, with the conceited wooing of Pandarus Prince of Licia. Written by William Shakespeare."

The habit of reprinting titlepages in order to make a book appear up to date was also, of course, common. One of the most interesting cases is that of the *Tragical Reign of Selimus* which originally appeared anonymously from the press of Thomas Creede in 1594, the unsold copies being re-issued more than forty years later, namely in 1638, as printed " by Iohn Crooke for Richard Serger," the new titlepage also bearing T. G. as the author's initials, no doubt with the object of leading the public to suppose that it was from the pen of Thomas Goffe, whose tragedies on oriental and classical themes had then lately appeared. The reverse case, that of two distinct editions in which the titlepages alone are printed from the same setting up of the type, though naturally far less frequent, nevertheless occurs, and is rather difficult to explain, since it is not easy to see why the titlepage should have been kept in type after the rest had been distributed. One instance, I think, occurs in the two editions of the anonymous comedy *Albumazar*, printed in 1615. The editions are certainly distinct, having collations respectively A² B-L⁴ and A-I⁴, but so far as I am aware the titlepages are identical. Since, however, I only know of one library which contains copies of both editions (U.L.C.), I should be inclined to suspect that one copy had the title properly belonging to the other edition, were it not for the fact that the identical case repeats itself in connection with the *Return from Parnassus*, copies of the two editions of which, published in 1606, may be compared both at the Bodleian and at Trinity College, Cambridge. Here we find that while the two editions have respectively the collations A-H⁴ I² and A-H⁴, the titlepages are again printed from the same setting up of the type. There is even a third case in the 1609 *Pericles* (*see* Addenda and Corrigenda, p. cxxviii), though here one of the editions is unfortunately represented by a single copy, the proper titlepage to which may have perished and been replaced from a copy of the other edition.

All bibliographers, and most editors, are of course familiar with the practice which obtained among the old printers of keeping works in type for a considerable period, and making alterations and corrections in the text during the then lengthy process of printing off. Of this practice the first quarto of *Lear* is the classical example, no two out of the six known copies agreeing throughout.* Another example typical of a large class is the *Revenger's Tragedy*, which originally appeared with the date 1607. In the course of printing off, however, several corrections were made in the text, and the later copies bear date 1608. In these cases it is often most difficult to decide whether we are merely to assume that 'copies differ,' or to recognise a different issue or even edition. I may mention that in my *List*, no notice has been taken of mere corrections in the text, while on the other hand a change of date or imprint, or any alteration amounting to a resetting of an appreciable portion of the type, has been held to constitute a separate issue. The practice reached its climax in the case of Jasper Mayne's *City Match*. This comedy was printed as a quarto in 1658 and issued along with the *Amorous War*. The following year it was deemed advisable to republish it as an octavo, and the type not having been distributed was rearranged with that view, not only the distribution of the pages being altered in the frame, but three lines from the bottom of the first page of the text being transferred to the top of the second, six from the bottom of the second to the top of the third, and so on throughout, the titlepage and some of the preliminary matter alone being reset. A similar though simpler case occurs in Carlell's *Passionate Lovers*

---

* Though I have quoted two Shakespearian quartos as well known examples of prevalent practices, it is not my intention to go into the bibliographical questions connected with his works. Many of these are matter of common knowledge, while the very complicated problems connected with the folios I regard as the special preserve of Mr. Sidney Lee.

of 1655. Here the octavo issue appears to be the earlier, and the pages to have been subsequently re-arranged as a quarto. No alteration of the type was made, and the page of print is rather small for the quarto size.

Of this habit of correcting the text while a work was printing off, there is, however, no more interesting case than that of the first folio of Ben Jonson's works, though so far as I know, no notice has ever been taken of it, beyond a few obvious points occurring on the titlepages to the various parts. Not only did the volume in question undergo careful revision in proof, no doubt at the author's own hands, but after the bulk of the edition had been printed off, many further corrections and alterations, in some cases involving the resetting of whole pages, were made, which are only presented in a very few copies. One of these is the magnificent copy on large paper preserved in the Grenville collection in the British Museum. The distinctive features of the two issues can perhaps best be illustrated by a comparison of this with the small paper Museum copy (C. 39. k. 9) which belongs to the more usual uncorrected issue. For convenience sake, I shall refer to the two copies as L.P. and S.P. respectively.

The first divergence to be noted occurs in the engraved title page to the volume. The imprint in the S.P. copy runs : " London | printed by W : | Stansby, and are | to be fould by | Rich : Meighen." In the L.P. copy this has been erased and re-engraved as follows : " Jmprinted at | London by | Will Stansby." The titlepages appear, however, to be distinct from the rest of the volume, either titlepage being found with either text, since of two copies preserved, one in the University Library and the other in the Library of Trinity College, Cambridge, in both of which the text usually agrees with S.P., the former has the long and the latter the short imprint. In the text, the differences begin with *Every Man out of his Humour*, the titlepage to which, sig. G1, has a woodcut border in the S.P. copy, which is absent in the L.P., the letterpress likewise being reset in larger type. The verso is blank in both cases, but the recto of G2, which has no number in S.P., is in L.P. paged 81, should be 76. The subscription to the dedication on the same page has also been reset,

S.P. reading : " By your true Honorer, Ben. Ionson," which in L.P. is altered to : " By your honourer, Ben. Ionson." From G5 onwards several pages have been corrected and partially reset, three lines from the foot of G5^r being moved to the top of G5^v, and two lines from the foot of G5^v to the top of G6^r. Also on G5^v a stage-direction occupying one line of text has been omitted. Several other directions throughout the volume have likewise been omitted, but in these cases merely from the margin. A casual inspection also reveals alterations in the text and partial resetting of the type at signatures G6^v, L6^r, O6^r, 2Y1^r–2Y4^v, 2Y6^r, and again on the last two pages of the volume, where in the Masque of *The Golden Age Restored*, the two songs after the dance with the ladies are transposed. In addition to these differences, the L.P. copy omits the words " for Matthew Lownes " from the imprint on the separate titlepage to *Poetaster*. The titlepage to *Cynthia's Revels* presents difficulties, for both the L.P. and S.P. copies in the Museum agree in having a plain titlepage, while both the Cambridge copies above mentioned have a woodcut border. Both copies preserved in the Bodleian exhibit points of interest. Thus the engraved titlepage to the Douce copy has an imprint different from either given above. It runs : " LONDON | Printed by | William Stansby." Again, while agreeing as elsewhere with S.P. in having Lowndes' name on the titlepage to *Poetaster*, it differs in having an ornamental woodcut border. The other copy (Art. A.A. 83) is interesting as representing a transition stage of sheet G, the text being uncorrected except as regards the omission of the stage-direction on 5^v. It is evident that the alterations were from the S.P. to the L.P. text, not only on account of the nature of the changes themselves, but from the fact that irregularities in the type in S.P., when not deliberately set right, appear on the whole exaggerated in the L.P., proving this to be the later of the two. The volume was reprinted in 1640. In all crucial cases the reprint follows the corrected text, except in the case of the subscription to the dedication on G2. This, then, would appear to be a late correction made after the bulk of the others, and not found in all copies of the corrected text.*

---

* The 1640 reprint includes one epigram not in the 1616 edition, which must have been added from MS., since it is dated 1629.

After Jonson's death on August 6, 1637, the question of an edition of his uncollected works naturally arose. The fate of his papers, from which the second volume of the 1640 edition was mostly printed, was long uncertain. Gifford wrote: "Into whose hands his papers fell, as he left, apparently, no will, nor testamentary document of any kind, cannot now be told; perhaps, into those of the woman who resided with him, as his nurse, or some of her kin; but they were evidently careless or ignorant and put his manuscripts together in a very disorderly manner, losing some and misplacing others." In 1659, however, the well-known publisher, Humphrey Moseley, issued by way of supplement to the 1658 edition of Suckling's *Fragmenta Aurea*, a volume entitled *The Last Remains of Sir John Suckling*, containing *inter alia* an unfinished tragedy, *The Sad One*, concerning which he wrote in the address to the reader as follows: "Nor are we without a sufficient President in Works of this nature, and relating to an Author who confessedly is reputed the Glory of the English Stage (whereby you'll know I mean Ben: Johnson) and in a Play also of somewhat a resembling name, *The Sad Shepherd*, extant in his Third Volume; which though it wants two entire Acts, was nevertheless judg'd a Piece of too much worth to be laid aside, by the Learned and Honourable Sir Kenelme Digby, who published that Volume." We are, therefore, justified in assuming that Sir Kenelm Digby at least prepared the papers for the press, and though this may not have amounted to much, I may mention that the text of the volume is in a very much better condition than Gifford's violent and uncritical abuse would lead one to suppose. On the other hand the volume bristles with bibliographical difficulties.* In the first place it contains three plays "printed by I.B. [*i.e.*, John Beale] for Robert Allot" as early as

---

* Mr. Brinsley Nicholson contributed an article on "Ben Jonson's Folios" to *Notes and Queries*, June 18, 1870, in which he compared the results of his investigations with the statements of Gifford and Lowndes. It is a careful piece of work, based on a minute examination of a certain number of copies, but to discuss his corrections and errors here would but further confuse an already intricate subject. I can only say that the article does not contain, as Mr. Hazlitt in the Catalogue of the Huth Library asserts, "all that can be said on the subject." For instance, Nicholson was unaware of the existence of the corrected issue of 1616.

1631, though there is no definite evidence of their having been published at that date. These are *Bartholomew Fair*, *The Staple of News*, and *The Devil is an Ass*, of which the second alone appears on the books of the Stationers' Company, being entered under date of April 14, 1626, to J. Waterson, though no edition by him is known. The above is the order in which the plays are given on the general title of 1640, and is also that in which they are most commonly found. Strictly speaking, however, the second and third should change places, since *Bartholomew Fair* ends with sig. M4 (p. 88), and is consequently continuous with the *Devil is an Ass*, which begins on sig. N1 (p. 91, two pages being skipped in the numbering). The *Staple of News*, on the other hand, has signatures 2A-(2)I6 (pp. 1–76). This arrangement actually occurs in one of the B.M. copies (C. 28. m. 12). It should be further noticed that each play has a separate titlepage, and that that of *Bartholomew Fair* occupies sig. A2. Of A1 I have been unable to discover any trace, and therefore cannot say whether it was blank or not. Its place was, of course, supplied, when the plays were included in the 1640 folio, by the general titlepage to that volume, so that the irregularity is not at first sight apparent. It is, therefore, not impossible that A1 may have been a general titlepage to these plays, and that they were intended as a supplement to the folio of 1616.* This suggestion receives some slight support from the titlepage of 1640 which, while stating that the volume contains "these Plays, Viz. 1 Bartholomew Fayre. 2 The Staple of Newes. 3 The Divell is an Asse," makes no reference to the other plays, masques, etc., included. Is it possible that the printer of 1640 followed, to some extent at least, a lost titlepage of 1631? Possibly further search through the imperfectly known treasures of our

---

* This theory is not invalidated by the letter quoted by Nicholson, in which Jonson, apparently referring to the three plays in question, complains of the printer, to whose remissness he ascribes the fact that more is not already in type, nor again by the likelihood of the ill-success of the *New Inn* having caused the publication to be suspended. Very likely a second volume was then in contemplation, and this project falling through, such matter as was in type may have been issued as a supplement to the 1616 volume. This view receives support from the fact of a certain number of copies having been printed on large paper to range with those of the former edition. One of these is in the library of Mr. Huth.

public and private libraries may yet be rewarded by the discovery of a perfect copy of the sheets as they issued from the press in 1631, but as yet all search has, so far as I am aware, proved vain.

The remainder of the volume, in which the plays included all appeared for the first time,* was set up in three sections, the order of which presents some difficulty. One section contains the *Magnetic Lady, Tale of a Tub,* and *Sad Shepherd,* and has sigs. A-P⁴ Q² R-V⁴ (pp. 1–156 with various misprints); another the *Masques, Underwoods,* and the fragment of *Mortimer,* with sigs. B-Q⁴ R² S-X⁴ Y² Z-2O⁴ 2P² 2Q⁴ (pp. 1–292); a third *Horace, his Art of Poetry,* the *English Grammar* and *Discoveries* with sigs. A-K⁴ L² M-R⁴ (pp. 1–132). This is the order in two copies in my possession and in one in the British Museum (79. 1. 4) while two other Museum copies (C. 39. k. 9, and C. 28. m. 12) agree in placing the *Masques* section before the *Magnetic Lady.* Some light may be gained from the folio of 1692. In the first place it may be mentioned with regard to the three plays of 1631 that this folio not unnaturally follows the order of the title-page of 1640, and places the *Devil is an Ass* before the *Staple of News.* With regard to the rest of the volume, it alters the order of works within one of the above mentioned sections, placing the *Masques* after *Underwood* and *Mortimer.* This is, of course, out of the question in the case of the 1640 folio. Otherwise, the sections themselves are in the same relative order as above given, namely *Magnetic Lady* section, *Masques* section, *Horace* section. This, then, I am inclined to regard as the correct order. But it will be further noticed that the second (*Masques*) section begins with

---

* In this connection I should like to remark that Mr. Fleay repeatedly asserts in his *Biographical Chronical* that *The New Inn* appeared in the present volume. Mr. Hazlitt makes the same statement, both in his *Handbook to Old English Literature* and his *Manual of Old English Plays.* It is utterly without foundation in fact, the play in question having been published in 8vo in 1631, and not being reprinted till the folio of 1692, where it appears at the very end of the volume, followed only by the *Leges Conviviales.* I speak from experience when I say that careless misstatements of this kind add enormously to the labour of subsequent investigators.

F

signature B,* and furthermore I may add that the recto of B1 is more or less soiled in all the copies, amounting to at least a dozen, that I have had an opportunity of examining. This part must therefore have lain folded and exposed to the dust for some time before the volume was finally made up, which suggests that it was printed first and had to wait for the others, a suggestion borne out by the fact that both the other groups contain special titlepages dated 1641, while the two in the second group agree in the date 1640. If, then, the second group was printed first, it was probably originally intended to follow immediately upon the 1631 plays (as we find it in the two Museum copies above mentioned), or even to begin the volume, in either of which cases the titlepage and any preliminary matter would naturally belong to this part. If no copy for these was supplied, the printer would very likely begin with signature B so as to leave A for such additional matter. This we see is exactly what he has done ; and so I conjecture that the sheet A of the second section is really represented by the general title-page to the volume.

And so at last, probably not till the spring of 1641, the volume appeared, from the press, it would seem, of B. Alsop and T. Fawcet, whose device is found on the title. But its adventures were not yet at an end. During the course of the year, the stock of the Allot plays of 1631 gave out. Thereupon the publisher, Richard Meighen, caused the *Devil is an Ass* to be reprinted alone and prefixed to the remainder of his edition of the rest of the volume. For this purpose he employed, not Alsop and Fawcet, but T. Harper, whose device appears upon the titlepage, though the imprint, dated 1641, mentions neither printer nor stationer. The general title, since it mentioned the three plays by name, had, of course, to be suppressed. It is difficult to make an estimate on such a point which shall have any value, but there must have been a considerable number of copies of this issue put forth, certainly I should think a quarter of the entire edition. They are not much 'esteemed,' being usually regarded as imperfect, and though for this

---

* My attention was first called to this point some time ago by Mr. Gordon Duff.

reason seldom found in collections are not uncommon in the second hand market. I am convinced, however, that this is a genuine issue, and that the copies appear as they did when they left the stationer's shop.*

There are certain variations in point of detail in the 1640–41 portion of the volume, which make it probable that the type was standing for some time, and that the whole of the edition was not printed off at once. Thus of three copies in my possession one has the word "Finis" at the end of the *Tale of a Tub*, and the words "Left unfinished" at the end of *Mortimer*, while the other two agree in omitting the "Finis" in the former case, and in reading "Hee dy'd, and left it unfinished" in the latter. Of the Museum copies one has the "Finis" while two have not, but all three agree in having the longer note at the end of *Mortimer*.

A similar case of the reprinting of a portion of a book occurs in works of Thomas Randolph. The only play of his which appeared during his life was the *Jealous Lovers*, a comedy acted by the Students of Trinity College before Charles and Henrietta Maria in 1632, and which appeared the same year "Printed by the Printers to the Universitie of Cambridge." The volume was a quarto, and was reprinted, again in quarto, in 1634, the year of Randolph's death, after which his works were collected by his brother Robert and printed by the printers to the University of Oxford in quarto in 1638. The *Jealous Lovers*, however, being the property of the Cambridge printers, as well as *Aristippus*, which had already appeared in London, were not included in the volume. In 1640 the works were reprinted in octavo, and the same year an octavo edition of the *Jealous Lovers* was issued at Cambridge. The two are often found bound up together, and it is not unlikely that they were issued by mutual agreement, but I do not consider that they form one publication. No mention is made of the *Jealous Lovers* on the titlepage

---

* Nicholson supposed that it was the stock of *Devils* alone that ran out, and assumed an issue containing two plays of 1631 and one of 1641. It is, however, inherently unlikely that the stocks of the three Allot plays should have varied, and I am not aware that any copy in the state assumed has ever been recorded.

of the Works, the words "The second Edition Enlarged" more likely referring to the fresh poems that were added to this edition. The play at least occurs separately, a copy being in the University Library at Cambridge, while nothing can be argued from the fact of their being found together, since the *Jealous Lovers* of 1632 or 1634 are frequently found bound up with the works of 1638, of which they are necessarily independent. In any case, the edition of the play outlasted that of the Works, and the surplus stock seems to have come into the hands of a piratical London stationer—Richard Royston apparently—who reprinted the Oxford volume in 1643 as "The Third Edition inlarged. Whereunto is added, *The Jealous Lovers*," carefully suppressing both his own and the printer's name, and adding the Cambridge *Jealous Lovers* of 1640. The volume, which is detestably bad alike as regards text and typography, does not seem to have gone off very rapidly, for it took three years to exhaust the stock of *Jealous Lovers*. This play was then reprinted and bound up with the remaining sheets of the rest of the volume. This reprint, however, is not common ; Mr. Hazlitt, who edited Randolph in 1875, knew of it, but the only copy I have seen is one in my own possession. It is badly executed, very much in the style of the rest of the 1643 volume, and is "Printed for Richard Royston, at the Angel in Ivie Lane, 1646."

I said above that the publisher of the 1643 volume suppressed both his and the printer's name, which is true, but on the separate titlepage to *Amyntas*, he preserved the Oxford imprint, and also the original date, 1640. This perplexing habit of reprinting imprints sometimes produces very startling results. Since the publication of my *List of Plays*, there has come into my possession an edition of "The Works of Sir Iohn Suckling. . . . Printed for Henry Herringman at the Anchor in the Lower Walk of the New Exchange, 1676." I can find no record of such an edition,* nor indeed of any edition between the *Fragmenta Aurea* of 1658 (with its

---

* Except as mentioned among the collected editions of Suckling at the end of Halliwell's *Dictionary* (copied in Hazlitt's *Manual*). It is not mentioned in Lowndes, in Hazlitt's *Handbook* or *Collections and Notes*, or his edition of Suckling, nor is it in the British Museum.

supplement, the *Last Remains* of 1659), and the *Works* of 1696. At first sight, I supposed the volume to be made up of parts of different editions with a new titlepage prefixed, but a closer examination showed it to be a genuine edition with separate titlepages reprinted from various earlier editions published by Humphrey Moseley. Thus the *Poems* are dated 1648, the three plays, *Aglaura, The Goblins* and *Brennoralt,* 1658, *The Last Remains* (reprinted with separate signatures as in the original issue) 1659. The titlepage to the alternative version of Act V of *Aglaura,* on the other hand, is "Printed for H. H. 1672," the whole, as I have said, being preceded by a general titlepage dated 1676. This is the first complete edition of Suckling's works, and it is, I think, the wildest piece of book-making from the bibliographical point of view that I have yet had the pleasure of coming across.

I hope that in the course of the above discussion I may have been able to throw a little light on certain bibliographical problems connected with the English drama, but it must be understood that it has rather been my object to take typical cases than to attempt an exhaustive inquiry. There are many points of interest on which I have not touched ; I will only here mention the order of the commendatory verses to *Cartwright's* plays published in 1651, as well as the cancel in the poems in the same volume, and the order of the sections in the folio editions of *Cowley's* works, while many other puzzles will at once occur to the mind of those who have devoted any attention to the subject. I may add that there are certain questions of detail in connection with the 1692 folio of Ben Jonson's works which I have not touched upon above. Perhaps some ingenious bibliographer will explain, *inter alia,* why sheet 3C of that volume is, as I believe, invariably discoloured ?

APPENDIX I.

ADVERTISEMENT LISTS.

APPENDIX I.

ADVERTISEMENT LISTS.

The following are reprints of the dramatic items from some old stationers' advertisements, together with notes showing the use that can be made of them. The collection is by no means complete, consisting only of some specimen lists occurring in dramatic publications, taken by way of illustration. For this purpose I have selected four of Moseley's, ranging from 1650 to 1654, six of Leake's from 1652 to 1660, one of Bedell & Collins' dated 1656, and one of Crooke's dated 1661.

HUMPHREY MOSELEY. I. 1650.

Joseph Rutter. *The Cid.* W. Wilson for H. Moseley. 1650 12°

Sig. D4.] *Courteous Reader,* These Bookes following are Printed for Humphrey Moseley, and are to be sold at his shop at the *Princes Armes* in St. *Pauls* Church-yard.

Sig. D5ᵛ.] Choyce POEMS, with Excellent Translations, and Incomparable Comedies and Tragedies, written by severall Ingenious Authors. [Nos. 1–30.]
  Included in Moseley's List II, 1653.

HUMPHREY MOSELEY. II. 1653.

Richard Brome. *Five New Playes.* for H. Moseley, Richard Marriot, and Thomas Dring. 1653. 8°.
  One sheet of advertisements at the end, signed A.

Sig. A1.] Courteous Reader, These Books following are printed for *Humphrey Mosely,* and are to be sold at his Shop at the *Prince's Armes* in St. *Paul's* Church-yard.

Sig. A3ᵛ.] *Choice Poems, with excellent Translations, and incomparable Comedies and Tragedies, written by several ingenious Authors.* [Nos. 54–103.]

Sig. A6.] *Books newly printed this present year for* Humphrey Moseley. [Nos. 104–117.]

Sig. A7.] *Books printed this Tearm for* Humphrey Moseley. [Nos. 118–129.]

Sig. A8.] *These Books I have now in the Presse, ready to come forth.* [Nos. 130–135.]

> All included in Moseley's List IV, 1654.

HUMPHREY MOSELEY. III. 1653.

Thomas Middleton. *The Changeling.* for H. Moseley, 1653. 4°. [4 entries.]

Sig. I3ᵛ. *PLAYES newly Printed.*

> 1.] [See IV. 134.]
> 2.] [See IV. 135.]
>
> *PLAYES in the Press.*
>
> 3]. [See IV. 137.]
> 4]. Also, *The Spanish Gypsies.*

No doubt Middleton's "Spanish Gipsy" (*cf.* Ap. II). The edition of 1653, however, is by *I. G. for R. Marriot*, and the play does not appear in List IV of the following year. *Plays*, p. 80.

HUMPHREY MOSELEY. IV. 1654.

William Cavendish, Duke of Newcastle. *The Country Captaine, And the Varietie.* for H. Robinson and H. Moseley. 1649.

> One sheet of advertisements signed A, added later.

Sig. A1.] Courteous Reader, these Books following are printed for *Humphrey Moseley,* and are to be sold at his Shop at the *Prince's Armes* in St. *Paul's Church-yard.*

Various Histories, with curious Discourses in humane learning, &c. [Nos. 1–35.]

Sig. A2.] *Books in Humanity lately Printed.* [Nos. 36–46.]

Sig. A3.] *Severall Sermons, with other excellent Tracts in Divinity written by some most eminent and learned Bishops, and Orthodox Divines.* [Nos. 47–67.]

Sig. A4.] *Books in Divinity lately Printed.* [Nos. 68–75.]

Sig. A4ᵛ.] *Choice Poems with excellent Translations by the most eminent wits of this Age.* [Nos. 76–104.]

76. *Fragmenta Aurea*, a collection of all the incomparable Pieces written by Sr. *Iohn Suckling* Knight. 8°.

Moseley, I. 3 and II. 56. *for H. Moseley*, 1648. *Plays*, p. 113.

81. *Pastor Fido*, the faithfull Shepheard, a Pastoral, newly translated out of the Original, by Mr. *Rich. Fanshaw*, Esq ; 4°.

82. Poems, with a discovery of the Civil Warres of *Rome*, by Mr. *Richard Fanshaw*, Esq ; in 4°.

I. 7 and 8, II. 60 and 61. *R. Raworth* [*for H. Moseley*] 1647 and *for H. Moseley* 1648, the 'Poems' being added in the latter year. It appears from this entry that the play was published separately ; the 'Poems' cannot have stood alone, so that No. 82 must refer to the whole volume. The work falls outside the limits of the *List of Plays*.

85. Medea, a Tragedy written in Latine by *Lucius Annæus Seneca*, Englished by Mr. *Edward Sherburn* Esq ; with Annotations, 8°.

I. 11 and II. 64. *for H. Moseley*, 1648. Outside our limits.

88. Poems with a Masque by *Thomas Carew*, Esq ; Gentleman of the Privy Chamber to his late Majesty, revived and enlarged with Additions. 8°.

II. 99. *for H. M* [*oseley ?*]. *and are to be sold by J. Martin*, 1651. *Masques*, p. 3.

89. Poems of Mr. *John Milton*, with a Masque presented at *Ludlow* Castle before the Earle of *Bridgewater*, then president of Wales, 8°.

I. 13 and II. 66. *R. Raworth for H. Moseley*, 1645. *Masques*, p. 18.

90. Poems, &c. with a Masque called The Triumph of Beauty, by *James Shirley*, Gent. 8°.

I. 14 and II. 67. *for H. Moseley*, 1646. The volume contains three parts, *viz.*, "Poems, &c.," "Narcissus," "The Triumph of Beauty," each with separate signatures, pagination and titlepages. From the present entry, however, it would appear that they formed one publication. *Masques*, p. 23.

95. Poems written by Mr. *William Shakespeare*, Gent. 8°.

II. 91. *T. Cotes and are to be sold by I. Benson*, 1640.

Sig. A5ᵛ.] *Poems lately Printed.* [Nos. 105–107].

105 [*bis*]. Choice Poems with Comedies and Tragedies, by Mr. *William Cartwright* late student of Christ Church in *Oxford*, and Proctor of the University. The Aires and songs set by Mr. *Henry Lawes*, servant to his late Majesty in his publick and private Musick. 8°.

II. 100. *for H. Moseley*, 1651. *Plays*, p. 17.

Sig. A5ᵛ]. *Incomparable Comedies and Tragedies written by several Ingenious Authors.* [Nos. 108–133.]

108. Comedies and Tragedies written by *Francis Beaumont* and *John Fletcher*, never printed before, and now published by the Authors Originall Copies, containing 34 plays, and a Masque, Fol.

> I. 1 and II. 54. *for H. Robinson and H. Moseley,* 1647. *Plays*, p. 3.

109.	The Elder Brother	
110.	The Scornful Lady	
111.	The Woman Hater	*Francis Beaumont*
112.	*Thierry* & *Theodoret* 4°	by &
113.	*Cupids* Revenge	*Iohn Fletcher.*
114.	Mounsieur *Thomas*	Gent.
115.	The two Noble Kinsmen	

> 109.   II. 76. *for H. Moseley,* 1651. *Plays*, p. 10.
>
> 110.   II. 77. Two editions *for H. Moseley,* 1651. *Plays*, p. 6.
>
> 111.   I. 21 and II. 74. *for H. Moseley,* 1649. *Plays*, p. 4.
>
> 112.   I. 22 and II. 75. *for H. Moseley,* 1649. *Plays*, p. 9.
>
> 113.   II. 78. The latest known edition is by *A. M*[*atthewes?*], without bookseller's name, 1635. *Plays*, p. 5.
>
> 114.   II. 79.   *T. Harpur for I. Waterson,* 1639, re-issued with a new titlepage, as " Father's own Son," *for R. Crofts,* n.d. *Plays*, p. 10.
>
> 115.   II. 80.   *T. Cotes for I. Waterson,* 1634, and bears the names of Fletcher and Shakespeare on the titlepage. *Plays*, p. 9.

116. The Country Captain and the Variety, two Comedies written by a person of Honour.   12°.

> I. 26 and II. 87. *for H. Robinson and H. Moseley,* 1649. Of the first the booksellers appear to have bought up a foreign edition, since the separate titlepage bears the imprint *In s'Grave van Haghe* [? s'Graven Haag = The Hague]. *Samuell Broun,* 1649. The separate title to the "Variety" has Moseley's name alone. It is to this volume that the present list was added in 1654. *Plays*, p. 18.

117. The Sophy, a Tragedy written by Mr. *Iohn Denham,* Esq; Fol.

> II. 97. *R. Hearne for T. Walkley,* 1642. *Plays*, p. 35.

118. *Brennoralt* or the discontented Collonel, a Tragedy written by Sir *Iohn Suckling* Knight.   4°.

> The only known separate edition is that under the title of " The Discontented Colonell," *E. G*[*riffin?*]. *for F. Eagles-field,* n.d., while all the collected editions are 8vo. *Plays*, p. 113.

119. The deserving Favorite by Mr. *Lodowick Carlel.* 4°.

for M. Rhodes, 1629. Moseley subsequently issued an edition of his own in 1659. *Plays,* p. 16.

120. *Albovine* King of *Lombardy*
121. The Just Italian. 4°.
122. The Cruel Brother. 4°.
123. The Unfortunate Lovers
124. Love and Honour. 4.

} Sir *William* by *Davenant.*

120. II. 81. *for R. M[eighen?].* 1629. *Plays,* p. 28.
121. II. 82. *T. Harpur for I. Waterson,* 1630. *Plays,* p. 28.
122. II. 83. *A. M[atthews?]. for I. Waterson,* 1630. *Plays,* p. 28.

123. I. 23 and II. 84. *for H. Moseley,* 1649. Moseley evidently bought up the remainder of the former edition, *R. H[odgkinson?]. sold by F. Coles,* 1643, and issued the sheets with a new titlepage. *Plays,* p. 28.

124. I. 24 and II. 85. *for H. Robinson and H. Moseley,* 1649. *Plays,* p. 28.

125. The Sophister by Dr. Z. 4°.

I. 20, without any indication of authorship. II. 73. "by Dr. *S.*" Langbaine makes no suggestion as to authorship. Halliwell, following the *Biog. Dram.,* states that the play "is said to have been written by Dr. Zouch," a suggestion which becomes an assertion with Fleay and Hazlitt, though they give no authority. The ascription is, however, borne out by the present entry.

126. Revenge of *Bussy D. Ambois*
127. *Byrons* Conspiracy. 4°.
128. *Byrons* Tragedy.

} *Georg Chapman.*

126. *T. S[nodham?]. solde by I. Helme,* 1613. *Plays,* p. 20.

127 and 128. The two plays form one publication in the only known editions, the latest of which is *N. O[kes?]. for T. Thorpe,* 1625. *Plays,* p. 20.

129. Contention for Honour & riches
130. Triumph of Peace. 4°.

} *I. Shirley.*

129. II. 88. The only known edition is *E. A[llde?]. for W. Cooke,* 1633. *Masques,* p. 23.

130. II. 89. adds "a Masque presented by the four honourable Houses of Inns of Court before the *King,* and *Queens* Majesty at *Whitehall,* 1633." Four issues of the same edition appeared *for W. Cooke,* in 1633. *Masques,* p. 23.

131. The Dutchess of *Malfi* by *Iohn Webster.*

II. 90. *I. Raworth for I. Benson,* 1640. *Plays,* p. 118.

132. The Northern lass by *Richard Brome.*

The only known edition previous to 1654 is *A. Mathewes sold by N. Vavasour,* 1632. Subsequently an edition was published by Moseley's widow, *for A[nne?]. Moseley,* 1663. *Plays,* p. 14.

133.   The Cid, a Tragicomedy translated out of French into English by *Ioseph Rutter* Gent.   12°.

> I. 27 and II. 92.   This is the second edition of Part I, *W. Wilson for H. Moseley*, 1650.   The first edition of Pt. I had appeared, *J. Haviland for T. Walkly*, in 1637, and Part II, *I. Okes for S. Browne*, in 1640.   Moseley probably bought up the remaining copies of Part II to issue with his reprint of Pt. I; but he did not issue either a general titlepage or a new one to Pt. II, and his reprint is also found separate.   *Plays*, p. 91.

Sig. A6.]   *Plaies lately Printed.*   [Nos. 134–140.]

134.   The Wild-Goose-Chase a Comedy written by *Fr. Beaumont* and *Iohn Fletcher.*   Fol.

> II. 115 and III. 1.   *for H. Moseley*, 1652.   *Plays*, p. 11.

135.   The Widow, a Comedy by *Ben. Iohnson, Iohn Fletcher,* and *Thomas Midleton.*   4°.

> II. 116 and III. 2.   *for H. Moseley*, 1652.   *Plays*, p. 79.

136.   The Changling by *T. Midleton* and *W. Rowley.*

> II. 126. and contains List III.   *for H. Moseley*, 1653.   *Plays*, p. 79.

137.   Six new plaies.   1. The Brothers.   2. The Sisters.   3. The Doubt-full Heir.   4. The Imposture.   5. The Cardinall.   6. The Court-Secret, by *Iames Shirley* Gent.   8°.

> II. 130 adds: "Being all that ever the Author made for the Private house in *Black-Fryers*."   III. 3 adds: "being All that were Acted at the *Black-Fryers*: Together with the *Court-Secret*, written by the same Author, but never yet Acted." *for H. Robinson and H. Moseley*, 1653.   "The Doubtful Heir," however, though written for the Black-Friars' was performed at the Globe.

138.   Five new plaies.   1. A mad couple wel matcht.   2. The Novella. 3. The Court Beggar.   4. The Citty Wit.   5. The Damoiselle by *Richard Brome* Gent.   8°.

> *for H. Moseley, R. Marriot and T. Dring*, 1653.   *Plays*, p. 13.

139.   The Tragedy of *Alphonsus* Emperor of *Germany*, by *George Chapman.*   4°.

> *for H. Moseley*, 1654.   *Plays*, p. 21.

140.   Two Tragedies, viz. *Cleopatra* Queen of *Ægypt*, and *Agrippina* Empresse of *Rome*, by *Thomas May* Esquire.   12°.

> *for H. Moseley*, 1654.   Plays, p. 75.

Sig. A6ᵛ.]   *New and excellent Romances.*   [Nos. 141–158.]

Sig. A7.]   *Books newly printed this Terme for me Humphrey Moseley.* [Nos. 159–170.]

Sig. A8.]　*These Books I do purpose to print very speedily.* [Nos. 171–180.]

The last entry gives the date of the list, since it mentions "these present Times 1654."

N.B.—The large number of cases noted above in which no edition is known to have been issued by Moseley is remarkable. It would be impossible to suppose that in each case an edition by him has been lost—and it is also unnecessary. In many instances Moseley seems to have bought up the stocks of other booksellers when they left business ; he may have intended to issue new titlepages, as he actually did in the case of D'Avenant's *Unfortunate Lovers* (IV. 123), but if so he seldom appears to have carried out his intention. Thus we find two books published by J. Benson (IV. 95 and 131) who continued in business till 1652. Moseley probably took over the stock in that year, since the books appear in Lists II. and IV. (1653 and 1654), but not in List I. (1650). Again we find three books originally belonging to J. Waterson (IV. 114, 115, and 121). These also are first found in List II., whence it would appear that Moseley did not take them over immediately upon Waterson's leaving business in 1641. They very likely remain in the hands of some third party, probably Waterson's heirs, for ten years. In the case of one of these plays (IV. 114) there is a re-issue, with a new titlepage *for R. Crofts,* n.d. This must have been after Moseley possessed the stock, since the dates of Crofts' business are 1657 to 1664. Moseley himself seems to have died in 1660 or 1661, but the business was carried on by his widow, Anne Moseley, till 1664, in which year the play in question must have passed immediately to Crofts and have been re-issued that year. Again, two of Shirley's Masques (IV. 129 and 130) bear the name of W. Cooke, who left business in 1641. As they are first mentioned in List II., we must again suppose an intermediate possessor. Other instances are IV. 126, published by J. Helme, who left business in 1616, and IV. 127, published by T. Thorpe, who continued till 1625, neither of which, however, appear in Lists I. or II. ; also IV. 117, published by T. Walkeley, which appears in Lists II. and IV. Of Walkeley's publications none are later than 1652, except one dated 1658. This, however, is a reprint of a Peerage published by him in 1644 and I take it to be a case of reprinted imprint (see *Essay,* p. xx). Sometimes the stocks of certain plays appear to have been transferred to Moseley, although the original publisher continued in business. One case in point is IV. 118, which Moseley was probably obliged to purchase of F. Egglesfield in order to have the right of the play for his collected edition of 1646 ; another is IV. 123, which he obtained from F. Coles, and which is the only case, as far as we know, in which he supplied a new titlepage. In two other cases, namely, IV. 119, published by M. Rhodes, who ceased publishing in 1629, and IV. 132, published by N. Vavasour, who continued till 1643, subsequent editions appeared, in the former case for Moseley himself in 1659, in the latter for his widow in 1663. In neither case, however, does the play appear to have come into Moseley's hands directly, being included in List IV. only. In the case of IV. 120, which was published by R. Meighen [?] in 1629, and which appears first in List II., the play must have been taken over from Meighen's successors (see note to Bedell's List, 1656). The only person with whom Moseley seems to have been connected in publishing ventures is Humphrey Robinson. Their connection was, however, of a casual nature, and does not appear to have gone beyond the publishing of individual books. They first joined forces for the publication of Beaumont and Fletcher's unprinted plays (IV. 108) in 1647. In 1649 they issued the volume of the Duke of Newcastle's plays to the remaining copies of which List IV. was added in 1654, and also D'Avenant's *Love and Honour* (IV. 124). The only other joint venture seems to have been Shirley's *Six New Plays* in 1653 (IV. 137). It is noteworthy that in every case the book is dramatic; Robinson's name always stands first.

WILLIAM LEAKE. I. 1652.

William Shakespeare. *Merchant of Venice.* for W. Leake, 1652. 4°.

> This is a re-issue of an edition of 1637, but with a new titlepage, on the verso of which the list appears.

> Sig. A1ᵛ.] *These Books following, are Printed and solde by* William Leake *at the signe of the Crown in* Fleetstreet.

>> 16 entries. All the plays (6 entries) are included in Leake's subsequent Lists.

WILLIAM LEAKE. II. 1655.

F. Beaumont and J. Fletcher. *A King and no King.* for W. Leak. 1655. 4°.

William Shakespeare. *Othello.* for W. Leak. 1655. 4°.

> In both volumes the lists are printed from the same setting up of the type.

> *A King,* sig. I4ᵛ; *Othello,* sig. M4ᵛ.] Printed or sold by *William Leake,* at the signe of the Crown in Fleetstreet between the two Temple Gates :
> *These Bookes following*

>> 46 entries. All the plays (10 entries) are included in List VI.

>> N.B.—Occurring in two volumes of 1655, the list presumably belongs to that year ; it does not contain the *Prince d'Amour* (*see* List IV). On the other hand it bears some resemblances to List VI, such as the mention, in the *Christ's Passion* entry, of both Grotius' and Sandys' names (otherwise only in V and VI) and the inclusion of *Henry IV* (otherwise only in VI). There is, however, nothing impossible in the List having appeared in 1655.

WILLIAM LEAKE. III. 1660.

James Shirley. *The Wedding.* for W. Leake. 1660. 4°.

> Sig. A1ᵛ.] *Books printed or sold by* William Leak, *at the sign of the Crown in* Fleet-street, *between the two Temple-gates.*

>> 52 entries. All the plays (9 entries) are included in the subsequent Lists.

WILLIAM LEAKE. IV. 1660.

F. Beaumont and J. Fletcher. *The Maids Tragedy.* for W. Leake. 1650

> Sig I4ᵛ.] *Books Printed or sold by* William Leake, *at the sign of the Crown in* Fleetstreet, *between the two Temple-gates.*

>> 53 entries. All the plays (10 entries) are included in the subsequent Lists.

If the date on the titlepage is correct, which it may be, then the list was printed on the verso of the last leaf ten years later, for it contains the advertisement of "Le Prince d'Amour," *i.e.*, not D'Avenant's masque, but a romance that appeared in 1660.

WILLIAM LEAKE. V. 1660.

James Shirley. *The Grateful Servant.* for W. Leake. [1660?]. 4°.

Sig. I2ᵛ.] *Books Printed, or Sold by* William Leake, *at the Sign of the Crown in* Fleetstreet, *between the two Temple Gates.*

53 entries. All the plays (10 entries) are included in List V.

WILLIAM LEAKE. VI. 1660.

F. Beaumont and J. Fletcher. *Philaster.* for W. Leake. [1660?]. 4°.

Sig. A1ᵛ.] *Books printed or sold by* William Leake, *at the sign of the Crown in* Fleetstreet, *between the two Temple-gates.* [60 entries.]

40. A *Tragædy* written by the most learned *Hugo Grotius*, called CHRISTUS PATIENS) [*sic*] and translated into English by *George Sandys.*

Leake I. 16. "Christs Passion, a Tragedie, by *George Sands.*" II. 32. "A Tragedy of Christs Passion, waitten [*sic*] by the most learned *Hugo Grotius* and Englished by *George Sands.*" III. and IV. 26, without translator's name, V. 28. *I. L[egatt?]. sold by W. Leake,* 1640. Another issue, *I. Legatt* without bookseller's name, appeared the same year. *Plays,* p. 92.

PLAYES.

50.] The Wedding.

II. 40, IV. 53, V. 45. Contains List III. The latest known edition previous to 1655 is for *I. Grove* 1633. It is possible that Leake bought this up before issuing his own, *for W. Leake,* 1660. Grove continued in business till 1661. *Plays,* p. 106.

51.] Philaster.

I. 11, II. 39, III. and IV. 45, V. 46. *for W. Leake,* "fifth Impression," 1652, "sixth Impression," n.d. *Plays,* p. 8.

52.] The Hollander.

II. 41, III. and IV. 46, V. 47. The only known edition is, *I. Okes for A. Wilson,* 1640; a bookseller otherwise unknown. *Plays,* p. 41.

53.] The Merchant of *Venice.*

II. 46, III. and IV. 47, V. 48. Contains List I. *for W. Leake,* 1652. *Plays,* p. 99.

54.] The strange discovery.

I. 15, II. 45, III. and IV. 48, V. 49. Two editions, *E. G[riffin?]. for W. Leake,* 1640. *Plays,* p. 43.

G

55.] Maids Tragedy.

> I. 13, II. 42, III. and IV. 49, V. 50. *for W. Leake,* 1650. *Plays,* p. 6.

56.] King and no King.

> I. 12, III. and IV. 50, V. 51. Contains List II. *E. G[riffin?]. for W. Leake,* 1639, and *for W. Leake,* 1655. *Plays,* p. 7.

57.] *Othello* the Moor of *Venice.*

> II. 43, III. and IV. 51, V. 52. Contains List II. *for W. Leake,* 1655. *Plays,* p. 102.

58.] The grateful servant.

> I. 14, II. 44, III. and IV. 52, V. 53. Contains List V. *I. Okes for W. Leake,* 1637, and *for W. Leake,* n.d. *Plays,* p. 107.

59.] *Henry* the Fourth.

> II. 38. *J. Norton sold by H. Perry,* 1639. *Plays,* p. 98.

60.] Tragædy of *Hoffman.*

> *I. N[orton?]. for H. Perry,* 1631. *Plays,* p. 22.

> N.B.—Perry ceased publishing in 1644, and Leake had certainly acquired *Henry IV* before 1655, although it is omitted from List III–V.

Sig. A2ᵛ.] These Books are lately come forth, and are to be sold by *William Leake,* at the Crown in *Fleetstreet,* between the two Temple Gates. [5 entries.]

> N.B.—William Leake was in business from 1634 to 1674, I believe always alone. His shop was the *Crown* in Fleet Street, and he often used a crown as his device. He must be distinguished from the William Leake of the *Holy Ghost* in St. Paul's Churchyard, who was publishing from 1560 (or rather 1590?) till 1611.

GABRIEL BEDELL AND THOMAS COLLINS. 1656.

Thomas Goffe. *Three Excellent Tragedies.* for G. Bedell and T. Collins. 1656. 8°.

Sig. R5.] These Books are printed for, and sold by GA. BEDELL and THO. COLLINS, 1656., viz.

Books in folio. [16 entries.]

Sig. R5ᵛ.] *Books in Quarto.* [17 entries.]

Sig. R6.] *Playes.* [20 entries.]

1.] *The Divels an Asse,* by *Ben. Johnson.* in *Folio.*

> This can only refer, among extant editions of the play, to that prefixed in 1641 to the remaining sheets of the second vol. of 1640. This has neither printer's nor bookseller's name, but bears on the titlepage a device used at that date by the printer, T. Harper. The volume originally appeared in 1640 *for R. Meighen. Plays,* p. 56, and *Essays,* p. xviii.

2.] *The Marriage of the Arts*, in *Quarto*, by *Barton Hollyday.*

I. *Haviland for R. Meighen*, 1630. *Plays*, p. 54.

3.] *The Just General*, in *Quarto.*

A play by Cosimo Manuche, *for M. M[eighen?]. T. C[ollins?]. and G. Bedell*, 1652. It does not come within our limits.

4.] *The Bastard*, in *Quarto.*

A play by Cosimo Manuche, *for M. M[eighen?]. T. Collins and G. Bedell*, 1652. It does not come within our limits.

5.] *The Wits*

6.] *The Platonick Lovers*   Written by Sir *William*

7.] *The Triumphs of Prince D'Amour*,   *D'Avenant*, in *quarto.*
    a Mask.

for R. Meighen, the former two in 1636, and the last in 1635. Bedell and Collins issued an edition of the two plays together in 1665. *Plays*, p. 28 and 27, and *Masques*, p. 6.

8.] *The Faithful Shepherdesse*, by *John Fletcher* Gent.

for G. Bedell and T. Collins, 1656. *Plays*, p. 9.

9.] *The merry Wives of Windsor*, by *Shakespear*, in *quarto.*

T. *H[arper?]. for R. Meighen*, 1630. *Plays*, p. 100.

10.] *Edward the* IV. the first and second part, in *quarto.*

H. *Lownes*, without bookseller's name, 1626. *Plays*, p. 49.

11.] *Michaelmas Term*, in *quarto.*

T. *H[arper?]. for R. Meighen*, 1630. *Plays*, p. 77.

12.] *Fine Companion*, in *quarto.*

A. *Mathewes for R. Meighen*, 1633. *Plays*, p. 69.

13.] *The Phœnix*, in *quarto.*

T. *H[arper?]. for R. Meighen*, 1630. *Plays*, p. 77.

14.] *The Combat of Love and Friendship*, by Dr. *Mead.*

for M. M[eighen?]., G. Bedell, and T. Collins, 1654. *Plays*, p. 76.

15.] *The Martyr.*
            In *quarto.*
16.] *Horatius.*

Polyeuctes and *Horatius* translated from the French of P. Corneille by Sir W. Lower ; the former *T. Roycroft for G. Bedell and T. Collins*, 1655, the latter *for G. Bedell and T. Collins*, 1656. *Plays*, p. 63.

17.] *The Hectors*, or the False Challenge, in *quarto.*

An anonymous comedy ascribed by Winstanley to E. Prestwich, and printed *for G. Bedel, and T. Collins*, in 1655. It does not come within our limits.

18.] *The Raging Turk,* or *Bajazet the II.* ⎫
19.] *The Courageous Turk,* or *Amurath the I.* ⎪ Written by *Thomas Goffe,* Master of Arts, and Student of Christs Church *Oxford.* Newly reprinted, in *octavo.*
20.] The Tragedy of *Orestes,* ⎭

"Three Excellent Tragœdies." *for G. Bedell and T. Collins,* 1656, containing the present List. The separate editions of the plays had been printed in 1631, 1632, and 1633 for R. Meighen.

Sig. R6. *Books in octavo.* [20 entries.]

Sig. R6ᵛ. *Books in* 12° *and* 24°. [13 entries.]

N.B.—The number of editions mentioned in the above List printed *for R. Meighen* deserves notice. The explanation is that Bedell and Collins succeeded to his business, as is shown by the fact of some of their books being printed for *M. M., G. Bedell and T. Collins.* Who this M. M. was is shown by the occurrence of imprints such as *for Mercy Meighen and Gabriel Bedell,* whence we may conclude that M. M. was Richard Meighen's widow. Meighen himself seems to have started in business, together with Thomas Jones, in 1615, to have dissolved the partnership in 1620, and to have died about 1640. After an interval of a few years the business was revived by the widow, Mercy Meighen, in partnership with Gabriel Bedell, their first book appearing in 1646. In 1650 Thomas Collins was taken in as a third partner. The retirement or death of Mercy Meighen in 1654 seems to have caused some confusion in the business. Thus we find Bedell's name together with R. Marriot and T. Garthwait on the titlepage of the *Reliquiæ Wottonianæ* of that year, while Walter Montaigne's *Miscellanea Spiritualia* bears the imprint *for J. Crook, G. Bedell, and Partners.* Before the end of the year, however, Bedell and Collins appear to have settled down into partnership together, without any third party, and continued so till 1667. After this we lose sight of Bedell altogether, while his partner may perhaps be identified with the T. Collins who was in business with one J. Ford in 1671, and the Thomas Collins for whom a tract on the trial of Elizabeth Collier was printed in 1680. There were three other Collins in the booksellers' trade, a John, a Matthew, and a Richard, from whom he must be distinguished.

ANDREW CROOKE. 1661.

F. Beaumont and J. Fletcher. *Wit without Money.* for A. Crooke, 1661. 4°.

Sig. 13ᵛ.] Plays written by *Francis Beaumont,* and *John Fletcher, printed in Quarto.* [Nos. 1–17.]

1 *Wit without Money.*

for A. Crooke, 1661. Containing the present List. *Plays,* p. 11.

2 *Night walker: or, the Little thief.*

for A. Crook, 1661. *Plays,* p. 11.

3 *Opportunity.*

The play is Shirley's, and was published as such, *T. Cotes for A. Crooke and W. Cooke,* 1640, and re-issued with the imprint altered, *T. Cotes for A. Crooke,* n d. *Plays,* p. 109–110.

4 *Coronation.*

T. Cotes for A. Crooke and W. Cooke, 1640. *Plays,* p. 11.

5 *Scornfull Lady.*

Latest known edition, *for H. Moseley,* 1651. *Plays,* p. 6.

6 *Elder Brother.*

for H. Moseley, 1651, and without name, 1661. *Plays,* p. 10.

7 *Philaster.*

The latest known editions are Leake's ; *see* his List VI. No. 51.

8 *King and no King.*

Leake, List VI. No. 56, and without name, 1661. *Plays,* p. 7.

9 *Monsieur Thomas.*

For the latest known editions, *see* Moseley, List IV. No. 114.

10 *Rollo Duke of Normandy.*

i.e. "The Bloody Brother" as printed by *L. Lichfield* in 1640. *Plays,* p. 10.

11 *Rule a wife and have a wife.*

L. Lichfield, 1640. *Plays,* p. 11.

12 *Thierry and Theodoret.*

See Moseley, List IV. No. 112.

13 *Woman Hater.*

See Moseley, List IV. No. 111.

14 *Maids Tragedy.*

Leake, List VI. No. 55, and without name, 1661. *Plays,* p. 6–7.

15 *Knight ot'h* [sic] *Burning Pestle.*

The latest editions are two by *N. O*[kes ?]. *for I. S*[methwicke ?]., 1635. *Plays,* p. 5.

16 *Cupids Revenge.*

A. M[athewes ?]., without bookseller's name, 1635. *Plays,* p. 5.

17 *Noble Kinsman.*

T. Cotes for I. Waterson, 1634. *Plays,* p. 9.

N.B.—Crooke does not say that the above plays were published by him, so he probably kept the editions of other publishers on sale. His connection with Cooke (see No. 3), usually with Cotes as printer, seems to have been of a very casual nature. Thus we find their names together in imprints dated 1637, 1639 and 1640, while each was likewise issuing works on his own account. Cooke ceased publishing in 1641, probably between the two issues of the *Opportunity.*

APPENDIX II.

THE EARLY PLAY LISTS.

APPENDIX II.

THE EARLY PLAY LISTS.

The following list is compiled from the entries in the early catalogues brought under one alphabet, the order being approximately that in which the titles appear in the Indexes to my Lists of Plays and Masques, so that any individual piece may be readily referred to. The early catalogues, as before stated, are four in number, and appear respectively at the end of *The Careless Shepherdess*, published by Rogers and Ley in 1656, of *The Old Law*, published later in the same year by Archer, of *Tom Tyler*, which appeared in 1661, as a joint venture apparently, by Brook, Kirkman, Johnson, and Marsh, and finally of *Nicomede*, published by Kirkman alone in 1671, the last being a mere reprint of the 1661 list with additions. Of these the first two and the last are here reprinted *in extenso*, though not in the original order. As regards the 1661 list, variations from that of 1671 are noted whenever they amount to more than mere details of orthography, etc., and entries only found in the later list are marked with an asterisk. I have in every case given the date of the first edition, preceded by an asterisk when all editions previous to the lists are anonymous, and a reference to the page in my own lists, on which the piece in question is entered (*Pl.* standing for *Plays* and *Mq.* for *Masques*), and have also added brief notes where they appeared necessary. In the case of plays or masques lying beyond the limits of my lists, the notes are enclosed in square brackets. All notes are corrective or supplementary of the latest of the old entries, which may in other respects be taken as correct, except as regards the use of the letters (T, C, TC, etc.), indicating the nature of the play. Of these, as not coming within the scope of bibliography, no notice has been taken ; they are utterly without authority, and will be found properly assigned in Mr. Fleay's *Biographical Chronicle.* Lastly, I may mention that a few misprints, such as reversed letters, confusion of *f* and long *s*, italic *h* and *b* (almost indistinguishable in the old founts), comma and period, and similarly obvious mistakes of the compositor, have been silently corrected, and a few letters omitted in the originals have been inserted within square brackets. The misprints which have been retained will probably satisfy readers that nothing of any consequence has been altered. The originals are very largely without punctuation, the titles, authors' names, etc., being printed in different columns in the three later lists. Since with the present arrangement this might have led to confusion where none exists in the originals, it has been thought well to place a period (.) wherever required. The entries are all printed from transcripts made from the copies in the British Museum. The following are the titles and headings of the volumes containing the catalogues :—

ROGERS AND LEY'S LIST, 1656 :

THE | Careles Shepherdess. | A | TRAGI-COMEDY | Acted before the KING & QUEEN, | And at *Salisbury-Court*, with great | Applause. | Written by T. G. Mr. of Arts. | *Pastorem Tittere pingues Pascere opportet oves, deductum | ducere Carmen.* | With an Alphebeticall Catologue of all such Plays | that ever were Printed. | [ornament] | *LONDON*, | Printed for *Richard Rogers* and *William Ley*, | and are to be sould at *Pauls* Chaine | nere Doctors commons, | 1656.

(B.M. 644. e. 21.)

Heading of list :

An exact and perfect Catologue of all *Playes* that are Printed.

ARCHER'S LIST, 1656 :

THE | *Excellent Comedy, called* | THE OLD LAW : | OR | A new way to please you. | By { *Phil. Massinger.* / *Tho. Middleton.* / *William Rowley.*

Acted before the King and Queene at *Salisbury House*, | and at severall other places, with great Applause. | Together with an exact and perfect Catalogue of all | the Playes, with the Authors Names, and what are | Comedies, Tragedies, Histories, Pastoralls, | Masks, Interludes, more exactly Printed | then ever before. | *LONDON*, | Printed for *Edward Archer*, at the signe of the *Adam* | and *Eve*, in *Little Britaine*. 1656.

(B.M. 644. e. 86.)

Heading of list :

An Exact and perfect CATALOGUE of all the PLAIES that were ever printed ; together, with all the Authors names ; and what are Comedies, Histories, Interludes, Masks, Pastorels, Tragedies : And all these Plaies you may either have at the Signe of the *Adam and Eve*, in Little Britain ; or, at the *Ben Johnson's* Head in Thredneedle-street, over against the Exchange.

KIRKMAN'S FIRST LIST, 1661 :

TOM TYLER | AND | His Wife. | AN EXCELLENT OLD | PLAY, | AS | It was *Printed* and *Acted* about a | hundred Years ago. | Together, with an exact *Catalogue* of all the playes | that were ever yet printed. | *The second Impression.* | [ornament] | *LONDON*, | Printed in the Year, 1661.

(B.M. 643. d. 63.)

Heading of list :

A True, perfect, and exact Catalogue of all the Comedies, Tragedies, Tragi-Comedies, Pastorals, Masques and Interludes, that were ever yet printed and published, till this present year 1661. all which you may either buy or sell at the several shops of *Nath. Brook* at the Angel in *Cornhil, Francis Kirkman* at the *John Fletchers Head*, on the Back-side of St. *Clements, Tho. Johnson* at the Golden Key in St. *Pauls* Churchyard, and *Henry Marsh* at the Princes Arms in *Chancery-lane* near *Fleetstreet.* 1661.

NICOMEDE. | A | Tragi-Comedy, | Translated out of the French | OF | MONSIEUR CORNEILLE, | By *JOHN DANCER.* | As it was Acted at the Theatre-Royal | IN | DUBLIN. | Together with an Exact Catalogue of all | the English *STAGE-PLAYS* printed, till | this present Year 1671. | Licensed *Dec.* 16. 1670. *Roger L'estrange.* | *LONDON:* | Printed for *Francis Kirkman,* and are to be sold at his Shop | in *Thames-street* over against the *Custom-House.* 1671.

(B.M. 643. d. 75.)

Heading of list :

A True, perfect, and exact Catalogue of all the Comedies, Tragedies, Tragi-Comedies, Pastorals, Masques and Interludes, that were ever yet Printed and Published, till this present year 1671. all which you may either buy or sell, at the Shop of *Francis Kirkman,* in *Thames-street,* over-against the Custom House, *London.*

At the end of this list is found the following :

An Advertisement to the Reader.

It is now just ten years since I Collected, Printed, and Published, a Catalogue of all the *English* Stage-Playes that were ever till then Printed ; I then took so great care about it, that now, after a ten years diligent search and enquiry I find no great mistake ; I only omitted the Masques and Entertainments in *Ben. Johnsons* first Volume. There was then in all, 690. several Playes ; and there hath been, since that time, just an hundred more Printed ; so, in all, the Catalogue now amounts to (those formerly omitted now added) 806. I really believe there are no more, for I have been these twenty years a Collector of them, and have conversed with, and enquired of those that have been Collecting these fifty years. These, I can assure you, are all in Print, for I have seen them all within ten, and now have them all by me within thirty. Although I took care and pains in my last Catalogue to place the Names in some methodical manner, yet I have now proceeded further in a better method, having thus placed them. First, I begin with *Shakespeare*, who hath in all written forty eight. Then *Beaumont* and *Fletcher* fifty two, *Johnson* fifty, *Shirley* thirty eight, *Heywood* twenty five, *Middleton* and *Rowley* twenty seven, *Massenger* sixteen, *Chapman* seventeen, *Brome* seventeen, and *D'Avenant* fourteen ; so that these ten have written in all, 304. The rest have every one written under ten in number, and therefore I pass them as they were in the old Catalogue, and I place all the new ones last. I have not only seen, but also read all these Playes, and can give some account of every one ; but I shall not be so presumptuous, as to give my Opinion, much less, to determine or judge of every, or any mans Writing, and who writ best; but I will acquaint you with some of my Observations, and so conclude. He that was the first Play-writer, I find to be one *Heywood*, not *Thomas*, but *John Heywood*, who writ seven several Playes, which he calls Interludes ; and they are very old, being Printed with the first of our *English* Printing ; and he makes notable work with the then Clergy. And indeed, by only reading of Playes, I find that you may be acquainted with the humours of that present Age wherein they were written. Also by Playes alone you may very well know the Chronicle History of *England*, and many other Histories. I could enlarge much on this account, having for my own fancy written down all the Historical Playes in a succinct orderly method, as you may do the like ; I observe that Playes were not only written by professed Poets, but also by the best Scholars, and Persons of Honour and Eminency ; especially, in these last hundred Playes, and not only Male, but Female Writers ; there being seven of them in all, four whereof in these last hundred. Although there are but 806. Playes in all Printed, yet I know that many more have been written and Acted, I my self have some quantity in Manuscript ; and although I can find but twenty five of *Tho. Heywoods* in all Printed, yet (as you may reade in an Epistle to a Play of his, called *The English Traveller*) he hath had an entire hand, or, at least, a main finger in the writing of 220. and, as I have been informed, he was very laborious ; for he not only Acted almost every day, but also obliged himself to write a sheet every day, for several years together; but many of his Playes being composed and written loosely in Taverns, occasions them to be so mean; that except his *Loves Mistress*, and, next to that, his *Ages*, I have but small esteem for any others. I could say somewhat more of him, and of all the old Poets, having taken pleasure to converse with those that were acquainted with them, but will conclude thus; that as *John Heywood* was the first *English* Play-writer, so in my Opinion, one *Thomas Meriton*, who writ two Pamphlets, which he calls Playes, viz. *Love and War*, and the *Wandring Lover*, was the worst. And although I dare not be absolute in my Opinion, who is the best of this Age, yet I should be very disingenuous, if I should not conclude, that the *English* Stage is much improved and adorned with the several Writings of several persons of Honour; but, in my Opinion chiefly with those of the most accomplished Mr. *John Dreyden*.

Yours, *Fra. Kirkman.*

Be pleased to excuse the misplacing of 4 of *Ben. Johnsons* Entertainments in E. & the omission of this one Play.

Sr. Rob. Howard—The Great Favourite, or, the Duke of Lerma.—T.

FINIS.

Rogers and Ley, 1656.	Archer, 1656.	Kirkman, 1661 and 1671.	REMARKS.
Abrahams Sacrifice.	Abraham's sacrifice. T. *Theod. Beza.*	Abrahams Sacrifice.	From the French of Theodore Beza, by Arthur Golding. 1577. *Pl.* 42.
Acteon.	Acteon and Diana. C.	*Rob. Cox.* Acteon & Diana. I.	[*Acteon and Diana*, a droll by Robert Cox. 1656.]
	Adelphes in Terence. I. *Rich. Bernard.*	Adelphus in Terence. C.	In 'Terence in English.' 1598. Richard Bernard. *Pl.* 12.
Adrasta, or the womans spleen.	Adrasta. C. *John Jones.*	*John Jones.* Adrasta. C.	1635. *Pl.* 54.
		* *S. Tuke.* Adventures of five hours. C.	[*The Adventures of Five Hours.* From Calderon, by Sir Samuel Tuke. 1663.]
Agamemnons Tragedy.	Agamemnon. C.	*John Studley.* Agamemnon. T.	1566. *Pl.* 93.
Aglaura, *Suclin.*	Aglaura. C. *John Suckling.*	*Sr. John Suckling.* Aglaura. TC.	1638. *Pl.* 113.
Alaham, Lord Brooks.	Alaham. T. *Lord Brook.*	*Lord Brooks.* Alaham. T.	Fulke Greville, Lord Brooke. In the col. ed. 1633. *Pl.* 44.
	Albion. I.	Albion. I.	Possibly it is the same as *Albion Knight.* n.d. *Pl.* 138.
		Albion's Triumph. M.	Aurelian Townsend. 1631. *Mq.* 25.
Albovin King of *Lombardy*, by *Davenant.*	Albowine King of Lombards. T. *Will. Davenant.*	*Sir W. D'Avenant.* Albovine. T.	1629. *Pl.* 28.
Albumazar.	Albumazar. C.	Albumazar. C.	* Thomas Tomkis. 1615. *Pl.* 115. Rather John Tomkins.

Rogers and Ley, 1656.	*Archer,* 1656.	*Kirkman,* 1661 and 1671.	REMARKS.
Alchimist, *Johnson.*	Alchymist. C. *Ben. Johnson.*	*Ben Johnson.* Alchymist. C.	1612. *Pl.* 57.
Alexandrian Tragedy.	Alexandrian — T. Sir *William Alexander.*	*Lord Sterling.* Alexandrian Tragedy. T.	William Alexander, E. of Stirling. In the *Monarchicke Tragedies,* 1607. *Pl.* 1.
All fools, *Chapman.*	All Fools. C. *Geo. Chapman.*	*Geo. Chapman.* All Fools. C.	1605 *Pl.* 19.
All for mony.	All for money. C. *Tho. Lupton.*	*T. Lupton.* All for money. T.	1578. *Pl.* 63.
All's lost by lust, *Masinger.*	All's lost by Lust. C. *Will. Rowly.*	*Will. Rowley.* All's lost by lust. T.	1633. *Pl.* 90.
Alls well that ends well.	All's well that ends well. I. *Will. Shakespeare.*	*Will. Shakespear.* All's well that ends well. C.	In folio 1623. *Pl.* 94.
Alphonsus Emperor of Germany, *Chapman.*	Alphonsus Emp. of Germany. T. *George Chapman.*	*George Peele.* Alphonsus Emp. of Germany. T.	George Chapman. 1654. *Pl.* 21. Winstanley followed Kirkman in ascribing it to Peele, for which he is reproved by Langbaine. It is, however, generally agreed that it is not by Chapman.
Alphonsus King of *Aragon.*	Alphonsus King of Arragon. T.	*R. C.* Alphonsus King of Arragon. H.	Robert Greene. 1599. *Pl.* 44.
		*Ben. Johnson. Entertainments of the Queen and Prince at Althrope. E.	1604. *Mq.* 14.
		* Jo. Weston. Amazon Queen. TC.	[1667.]
Amends for Ladies.	Amends for Ladies. C. *Nath. Field.*	*Nat. Field.* Amends for Ladies. C.	1618. *Pl.* 36.

Rogers and Ley, 1656.	Archer, 1656.	Kirkman, 1661 and 1671.	REMARKS.
Aminta.	Aminta. T. *Torquato Tasso.* Tarquato Tasso. P.	*Torquato Tasso.* Aminta. P.	*From the Italian of Tasso, by John Reynolds. 1628. *Pl.* 89. The duplicate entry in Archer's list seems due to the title-page, which reads " Torquato Tasso's Aminta Englisht." The ascription to Reynolds rests on Phillips' authority.
		* *John Dancer.* Aminta. P.	[From the Italian of Tasso, by John Dancer. 1660.]
		*Amorous Orontus. C.	[John Bulteel. 1665.]
	Amorous War. T. *Jasper Mayne.*	*Dr. Maine.* Amorous War. C.	In the 'Two Plays,' 1658. *Pl.* 76.
		* Amorous Widow & wanton Wife. C.	[*The Amorous Widow, or the Wanton Wife.* Betterton. It was acted in 1670, but no edition earlier than 1706 is now known.]
Amintus, or the unpossile [*sic*] dowry.	Amintas, or the impossible dowry. C. *Tho. Randalph.*	*Tho. Randall.* Amyntas. C. 1661] *Randoll.*	*Thomas Randolph.* In 'Poems,' 1638. *Pl.* 86.
Andrew, Terence.	Andrea in Terence. C. *Rich. Bernard.*	Andrea in Terence. C. 1661] *Bernard.*	Richard Bernard. In 'Terence in English,' 1598. *Pl.* 12.
	Andrian woman. C. *Tho. Newman.*		*Andria.* With the *Eunuch,* 1627. *Pl.* 83.
		Andromana. T.	[J. S. 1660.]
		**John Wilson.* Andronicus Comnenius. T.	[1664.]
Antonio and Cleopatra.	Antonio and Cleopatra. T. *Will. Shakespeare.*	*Will. Shakespear.* Anthony & Cleopatra. T.	In folio 1623. *Pl.* 94.

Rogers and Ley, 1656.	*Archer,* 1656.	*Kirkman,* 1661 *and* 1671.	REMARKS.
Antigone, or the Theban Princes.	Antigone. T. *Tho. May.*	* *Tho. May.* Antigone. T.	1631. *Pl.* 75.
Antipodes, Brome.	Antipodes. C. *Rich. Brome.*	*Rich. Broome.* Antipodes. C.	1640. *Pl.* 14.
	Antiquary. C. *Shakerly Mermion.*	*Shak. Marmion.* Antiquary. C.	1641. *Pl.* 69.
Antonio and Melida, *Marston.*	Antonia and Melida. T. *John Marston.*	*John Marston.* Antonio & Melida. T. [Pt. II.]	1602. *Pl.* 70.
	Antonia's Revenge. T. *John Marston.*	*John Marston.* Antonio & Melida. T.	*Antonio's Revenge.* 1602. *Pl.* 70.
		Lady Pembrook. Antonius. T.	Mary Herbert (*see* Sidney) C. of Pembroke. 1592. *Pl.* 111.
		* *Tho. Middleton.* Any thing for a quiet life. C.	1662. *Pl.* 80.
Apollos shroving.	Apollo's shroving. C.	*E. W.* Apollo Shroving. C.	*William Hawkins, n.d. *Pl.* 46. The initials E.W. at the end of the preface are those of the person who caused the play to be printed.
		R.B. Appius & Virginia. T.	Author unknown (possibly Richard Bower). 1575. *Pl.* 123.
Apias and Virginia	Appius and Virginia. T. *John Webster.*	*John Webster.* Appius and Virginia. T.	1654. *Pl.* 119. The reference in Rogers' list is probably to Webster's play, though it may be noted that title to R. B.'s has "Apius."

Rogers and Ley, 1656.	*Archer,* 1656.	*Kirkman,* 1661 *and* 1671.	REMARKS.
Arcadia, *Sherly.*	Arcadia. C. *Iames Shirly.*	*James Shirley.* Arcadia. P.	1640. *Pl.* 109.
Arden of Feversham.	Arden of Feversham. I. *Rich. Bernard.*	Arden of Feversham. T.	Author unknown. 1592. *Pl.* 124.
Argulus and Parthenia. *Glapthorn.*	Argalus and Parthenia. C. *Hen. Glapthorn.*	*Hen. Glapthorne.* Argalus & Parthenia. P.	1639. *Pl.* 41.
Aristippus, *Randolph.*	Aristippus. T. *Tho. Randalph.*	*Tho. Randall.* Aristippus. I. 1661]. *Randoll.*	Thomas Randolph. 1630. *Mq.* 22.
Arraignment of Paris.	Arraignment of Paris. T. *Will. Shakespeare.*	*Will. Shakespear.* Arraignment of Paris. P.	*George Peele. 1584. The ascription rests on the authority of Nash's preface to Greene's *Menaphon.* 1590.
Arviragus and Philicia.	Arviragus & Philesia's 1. 2. part. T. Lodowick Carlile.	*Lod. Carlile.* Arviragus & Philicia, 1st. part. TC. *Lod. Carlile.* Arviragus & Philicia, 2d. part. TC.	1639. *Pl.* 16.
As you like it, *Shakspear.*	As you like it. C. *Will. Shakespeare.*	*Will. Shakespear.* As You like it. C.	In folio 1632. *Pl.* 94.
		Leonard Willan. Astrea. P.	[1651.]
Atheist Tragedy, *Cyril Teudor.*	Atheist. T. *Cyril Tourner.*	*Cyryl Turneur.* Atheists Tragedy. T.	1611. *Pl.* 116.
		Ben. Johnson. Masque of Augurs. M.	1621. *Mq.* 15.
	Baggs Seneca. T.		I can offer no suggestion as to the meaning of this entry.

H 2

Rogers and Ley, 1656.	*Archer,* 1656.	*Kirkman,* 1661 *and* 1671.	REMARKS.
Ball, *Sherly*.	Ball. C. *George Chapman.*	*James Shirley*. Ball. C.	Chapman & Shirley. 1639. *Pl.* 21.
	Band ruffe and cuffe. C.	Band, Ruff & cuff. I.	*Band, Cuffe and Ruffe.* 1615. *Mq.* 27.
Barthollomew faire, *Johnson*.	Bartholomew - fair. C. *Ben. Johnson.*	*Bed. Johnson*. Bartholmew Fair. C.	In vol. II of folio 1640. (1631.) *Pl.* 55.
	Bartholomew Fairing. C.		There are several works with this title, but they do not appear to be dramatic. (*See* Index to Hazlitt). It might, however, refer to some show presented at the fair.
	Bashfull lovers. C. *Philip Massinger.*	*Phil. Massenger*. Bashful Lover. C.	In 'Three New Plays,' 1655. *Pl.* 72.
Bastard a Tragidy.	Bastard. T. *Cosmo Manuche.*	Bastard. T.	[Cosmo Manuche. 1652.]
	Battel of Affliction. T.		Unless this is a misprint for "Battle of Affections," and is a duplicate entry of *Pathomachia*, I cannot identify it.
Battel of Alcazar, or the death of Stukely.	Battell of Alcazar. T.	Battle of Alcazar. T.	*George Peele. 1594. Attributed to Peele by Dyce on the ground of lines from it being ascribed to him in *England's Parnassus*. *Pl.* 84.
Bays.			
		Ben. Johnson. Queens Masque of Beauty. M.	*The Masque of Beauty.* In 'Two Royal Masques,' n.d. *Mq.* 14.
Beggers bush, *B*.	Beggers bush. T. *John Fletcher.*	*John Fletcher*. Beggars Bush. C.	In folio 1647. *Pl.* 3.

Rogers and Ley, 1656.	*Archer,* 1656.	*Kirkman.* 1661 *and* 1671.	REMARKS.
		Killigrew. Bella-mira her Dream.	Thomas Killigrew. In folio 1664. *Pl.* 59.
Bird in a cage, *Sherly.*	Bird in a Cage. C. *James Shirley.*	*James Shirley.* Bird in a Cage. C.	1633. *Pl.* 107.
		Shakespeare and Rowley. Birth of Merlin. TC.	1662. *see* William Rowley. *Pl.* 91.
		Earl of Orrery. Black Prince. T.	[1669.]
		Ben Johnson. Queen's Masque of Blackness. M.	*The Masque of Blackness.* In 'Two Royal Masques,' n.d. *Mq.* 14.
		Dut. of Newcastle. Blazing World. C.	[Unfinished. In 'Works,' 1668.]
Blinde begger of Alexandria.	Blind Begger of Alexandria. T. *George Chapman.*	*George Chapman.* Blind Beggar of Alexandria. C.	1598. *Pl.* 18.
		John Day. Blind Beggar of Bednal Green. C.	1659. *Pl.* 31.
		Sir Rob. Howard. Blind Lady. C.	[In 'Poems,' 1660.]
Bloody banquet. *T. D.*	Bloody banquet. T. *Thomas Barker.*	*T. D.* Bloody Banquet. T.	1620. *Pl.* 136.
Rollo Duke of Nor-mandy, *Fletcher.*	Bloody Brother. T. *John Fletcher.* Rollo Duke of Nor-mandie. T. *John Fletcher.*	*John Fletcher.* Bloody Brother. T.	*The Bloody Brother.* 'By, B. J. F.' 1639. (*Rollo Duke of Normandy.* Flet-cher. 1640.) *Pl.* 10.
Burt Mr. Constable.	Blurt Mr. Constable. T.	*Tho. Midleton.* Blurt Mr. Consta-ble. C.	1602. *Pl.* 77.

Rogers and Ley, 1656.	*Archer,* 1656.	*Kirkman,* 1661 *and* 1671.	REMARKS.
{ Bondman, *Messenger*. Bondman, *Fletcher*.	Bondman. T. *Phil. Massinger.*	*Phil. Massenger.* Bondman. C.	1624. *Pl.* 73.
Bonduca, *Fletcher*.	Bonduca. T. *John Fletcher.*	*John Fletcher.* Bonduca. T.	In folio 1647. *Pl.* 3.
Brazen Age.	Brazen Age. C. *Tho. Haiwood.*	*Tho. Heywood.* Brazen Age. C.	1613. *Pl.* 51.
Bride, *Thomas Nabs*.	Bride. C. *Thomas Nabbs.*	*Tho. Nabs.* Bride. C.	1640. *Pl.* 82.
		*Dut. of Newcastle. Bridals. C.	In 'Works,' 1668.
		*Sir W. D'Avenant. Britannia Triumphans. M.	1637. *Mq.* 6.
Broken Hart, *Ford*.	Broken heart. C. *John Foard.*	*John Ford.* Broken Heart. T.	1633. *Pl.* 37.
Brothers, *Sherly*.	Brothers. C. *James Shirly.*	*James Shirley.* Brothers. C.	In 'Six New Plays,' 1653. *Pl.* 106.
Bussey dambois.	Bussey D Amboys. T. *George Chapman.*	*Geo. Chapman.* Bussy D'Amboys. T.	1607. *Pl.* 19.
	Cæsars revenge. T.	Cæsar's Revenge. T.	*Caesar & Pompey or Caesar's Revenge.* 1607. *Pl.* 134.
Cambises King of Persia.	Cambises King of Persia. T. *Thomas Preston.*	*Tho. Preston.* Cambyses King of Persia. TC.	n.d. *Pl.* 86.
Alexander and Campaspe.	Alexandriæ—Campasnæ. T. *John Lilly.*	*John Lilly.* Alexander and Campaspe. C.	*Campaspe* or *Alexander, Campaspe, and Diogenes,* 1584. *Pl.* 64.
Captaine, *Beoment*.	Captain. T. *Iohn Fletcher.*	*John Fletcher.* Captain. C.	In folio 1647. *Pl.* 3.

Rogers and Ley, 1656.	*Archer,* 1656.	*Kirkman,* 1661 and 1671.	REMARKS.
Cardinall, *Sherly.*	Cardinal. C. *James Shierly.*	*James Shirley.* Cardinal. T.	In 'Six new Plays,' 1653. *Pl.* 106.
	Careless shepherd. C.	*Tho. Goffe.* Careless Shepherdess. TC.	1656. *Pl.* 42. Contains Rogers & Ley's list.
		*Tho. Porter. Carnivall. C.	[1664.]
Case altred, *Johnson.*	Case is altered. C. *Ben. Johnson.*	*Ben. Johnson.* Case is alter'd. C. 1661] The.	1609. *Pl.* 57.
Catelin, *Johnson.*	Catalines conspiracie. T. *Ben. Johnson.*	*Ben. Johnson.* Catilines Conspiracy. T.	*Cataline his Conspiracy.* 1611. *Pl.* 57.
Chabot Admirall of France.	Chabut Admiral. T. *Iames Shirly.*	*James Shirley.* Chabot Admiral of France. T.	George Chapman & James Shirley. 1639. *Pl.* 21.
		*Ben Johnson. Challenge at Tilt. M.	In folio 1616. *Mq.* 11.
Challenge for beuty.	Challenge for beauty. C. *Tohmas* [sic] *Heywood.*	*Tho. Heywood.* Challenge for Beauty. C.	1636. *Pl.* 53.
Chances, *Beamont.*	Chances. C. *Will Shakespear.*	*John Fletcher.* Chances. 1661] C.	In folio 1647. *Pl.* 3.
Changes, or love in a maze.	Changes, or love in a maze. C. *Iames Shirly.*	*James Shirley.* Changes, or Love in a Maze. C.	1632. *Pl.* 107.
Changling, *Middleton.*	Changeling. C.	*Midleton* & *Rowly.* Changling. C.	1653. *Pl.* 79.
	Characters. M.		Probably for *The Characters of Two Royal Masques* (i.e. *Blackness and Beauty.* q.v.)

Rogers and Ley, 1656.	*Archer,* 1656.	*Kirkman,* 1661 *and* 1671.	REMARKS.
King Charles Tragedy.		Charles the 1st. T.	[*The Famous Tragedy of King Charles the First basely butchered.* Anon. 1649.]
Chast Maid of Cheapside, *Middleton.*	Chaste maid of Chepside. C. *Thomas Middleton.*	*Tho. Midleton.* Chaste Maid in Cheapside. C.	1630. *Pl.* 79.
		*[John Wilson] Cheats. C.	[1664. The author's name added in MS.]
Promises of God manifested.	Promise of God manifested. I.	Promises of God manifested.	'A Tragedye or enterlude manyfestyng the chife promyses of God.' John Bale. 1577. *Pl.* 2.
Chinon of England.			Mentioned in Henslowe's *Diary,* Jan. 3. 1595-6 &c., and entered on the Stationers' Register, Jan. 20, but not now known.
	Chlaridiæ. T. [?]	*Ben. Johnson.* Cloridia, rites to Cloris. M.	Chloridia. n.d. *Mq.* 15.
		Geo. Sands. Christ's Passion. T.	1640. *Pl.* 92.
Christian turn'd Turk. *Daborne.*	Christian turned Turk. C. *Robert Daborne.*	*Dawbourne.* Christian turn'd Turk. T.	Robert Daborne. 1612. *Pl.* 25.
		Ben. Johnson. Christmas his Masque. M.	In Vol. II of folio 1640. *Mq.* 12.
M.T. Cicero.	Tullius Cicero. T.	Marcus Tullius Cicero. T.	[*Marcus Tullius Cicero.* Anon. 1651.]
Cid two parts.	Cid 1. 2, parts. C. *Ioseph Rutter.*	*Jos. Rutter.* Cid 1st. part. TC. *Jos. Rutter.* Cid 2d. part. TC.	Part I 1637. Part II 1640. *Pl.* 91.

Rogers and Ley, 1656.	*Archer,* 1656.	*Kirkman,* 1661 *and* 1671.	REMARKS.
		Phil. Massenger. City Madam. C. 1661] The	1658. *Pl.* 74.
City match.	Citie match. C. *Iasper Mayne.*	*Dr. Mayne.* City Match. C.	1639. *Pl.* 76.
		*Rob. Davenport. City Night-Cap. TC.	1661. *Pl.* 30.
City wit, *Brown.*	Citie wit. C. *Richs Benne.*	*Rich. Brome.* City Wit. C.	In 'Five new Plays,' 1653. *Pl.* 13.
Claracilla, *Killigrew.*	Claracilla. T. *Thomas Keligrew.*	*Tho. Killigrew.* Claracilla. TC.	With the *Prisoners,* 1641. *Pl.* 59.
Cleopatra Daniel.	Cleopatra. C. *Samuel Daniel.*	*Sam. Daniel.* Cleopatra. T.	In *Delia,* 1594. *Pl.* 25.
Cleopatra, *May.*	Cleopatra. T. *Tho. May.*	*Tho. May.* Cleopatra. T.	1639. *Pl.* 75.
Cleopatra.	Cleopatra. T. Samuell Daniel.		What Rogers' entry means I cannot say. Archer seems to have copied it and added the author's name, forgetting that he had already entered Daniel's play.
{ Knight of the Golden Shield. Cleomon Knight of the Shield.	Knight golden shield. C.	Knight of the Golden Shield. H.	*Sir Clyomon Knight of the Golden Shield & Clamydes the White Knight.* 1599. *Pl.* 129.
Coblers prophesies.	Coblers prophesies. C. *Robert Wilson.*	*Rob. Wilson.* Coblers Prophesie. C. 1661] The	1594. *Pl.* 121.
	Cœlum Britannicum. M.	*Tho. Carew.* Cœlum Brittanicum. M.	1634. *Mq.* 3.

Rogers and Ley, 1656.	Archer, 1656.	Kirkman, 1661 and 1671.	REMARKS.
Colas fury or Licendas misery.	Coolayes fury. T.		[*Colas Fury, or Lyrenda's Misery.* Henry Birkhead. 1646.]
Combat of love and friendship.	Combate of love. C. *Robt. Meade.*	*Rob. Mead.* Combat of Love & Friendship. C.	1654. *Pl.* 76.
Comedy of errors, *Shakepear* [*sic*].	Comedy of errrors. C. *William Shakespear.*	*Will. Shakespear.* Comedy of Errors. C.	In folio 1623. *Pl.* 94.
		* *Geo. Etherege.* Love in a Tub. C.	[*The Comical Revenge, or Love in a Tub.* 1669.]
		**Sir Rob. Howard.* Committee. C.	[In 'Four New Plays,' 1665.]
Committy man, *Currie.*	Committie-man cured. C.	[*S*] *Sheppard.* Committe-man curried. C.	[1647. The author's initial added in MS.]
Common conditions.	Common conditions. C.	Commons Conditions. C.	n.d. *Pl.* 138.
		Milton's Masque. M. 1661.] *John Milton.* Miltons Mask. M.	* *Comus.* 1637. *Mq.* 19.
Conflict of conscience, *Wood.*	Conflict of conscience. I. *Sam Wood.*	*Nat. Woods.* Conflict of Conscience. P.	1581. *Pl.* 121.
Biro's Conspiracy. *Chapman.*	Byron's Conspiracie. T. *George Chapman.* Byrons Tragedie. T. *George Chapman.*	Geo. Chapman. Byrons Conspiracy. H. Geo. Chapman. Byrons Tragedy. T.	*The Conspiracy and Tragedy of Charles Duke of Byron.* Two Parts. 1608. *Pl.* 20.

Rogers and Ley, 1656.	Archer, 1656.	Kirkman, 1661 and 1671.	REMARKS.
Constant maid.	Constant maid. C. *James Shirley.*	*James Shirley.* Constant Maid. C. **T.B.* Love will find out the way. C.	*The C. M.* 1640. (*Love &c.* T.B. 1661.) *Pl.* 109.
Liberality and prodigality.	Liberalitie and prodigalitie. C.	Liberality & Prodigality. C.	*The Contention between Liberality and Prodigality.* 1602. *Pl.* 130.
	Lancaster and York. H.		*The Contention betwixt the two famous Houses of York and Lancaster.* 1594. *Pl.* 125.
Contention for honour & riches.	Contention for honor and riches. M. *Iames Shirley.*	**James Shirley.* Contention of Honor & riches. M.	*The Contention for Honour and Riches.* 1633. *Mq.* 23.
		*Dut. of Newcastle. Covent of Pleasure. C.	*Convent of P.* [1668.]
Coriolanus, *Shakspear.*	Coriolanus. T. *William Shakespear.*	*Will. Shakespear.* Coriolanus. T.	In folio 1623. *Pl.* p. 94.
Cornelius Tragidy.	Cornelius. T. *Thomas Lloyd.*	*Tho. Kyd.* Cornelia. T.	1594. *Pl.* 60.
	Coroniæ Minervæ. M.		**Corona Minervæ.* Author unknown. 1635. *Mq.* 28.
Coronation, *Fletcher.*	Coronation. C. *Iames Shirley.*	*James Shirley.* Coronation. C.	John Fletcher, 1640. *Pl.* 11. Claimed by Shirley in his 'Six new Plays,' 1653. (sig. F 4.)
Costly whore.	Costly whore.	Costly Whore.	1633. *Pl.* 137.
Country Captaine.	Country Captain. T. *Will. E. of Newcastell.*	*Duke of Newcastle.* Country Captain. C. 1661] *Earl.*	William Cavendish, D. of N. With the *Variety* 1649. *Pl.* 18.

Rogers and Ley, 1656.	*Archer,* 1656.	*Kirkman,* 1661 and 1671.	REMARKS.
	Country Girle. C. *Thomas Brewer.*	*Ant. Brewer.* Coun trey Girle. C.	'By T. B.' 1647. *Pl.* 143.
Coragious Turk,	Couragious Turk. T. *Thomas Goffe.*	*Tho. Goffe.* Cour agious Turk. T.	1632. *Pl.* 42.
Court begger.	Court begger. C. *Richard Broome.*	*Rich. Brome.* Court Beggar. C.	In 'Five new Plays,' 1653. *Pl.* 13.
	Court secret. C.	*James Shirley.* Court Secret. C.	In 'Six new Plays,' 1653. *Pl.* 106.
Covent Garden.	Covent Garden. C. *Thomas Nabbs.*	*Tho. Nabs.* Cov ent Garden. C.	1638. *Pl.* 82.
		Rich. Brome. Wed ding of Covent-Garden, or the Middlesex Justice of Peace. C. 1661] The Wed ding . . . Justice of &c.	*Covent Garden (Weeded).* In 'Five new Plays,' 1659. *Pl.* 14.
Coxcomb, *Beamont.*	Coxcombe. C. *Iohn Fletcher.*	*John Fletcher.* Cox comb. C.	In folio 1647. *Pl.* 3.
		1661 only.] Crafty Cromwel. TC.	Unless this is a duplicate of *Cromwell's Conspiracy,* I cannot identify it. Its omis sion in 1671 suggests that it is a mistake of some kind.
Cressus Tragidy, *Sterlin.*	Cræsus. T. *William Alexander.*	*Lord Sterling.* Crœsus. T.	William Alexander, E. of Sterling. In the *Monarchick Tragedies.* 1604. *Pl.* 1.
Cromwells history.	Cromwells historie. H. *William Shakespere.*	*Will. Shakespear.* Cromwels History. H.	*Thomas Lord Cromwell.* 'Written by W. S.' Pseudo-Shak. 1602. *Pl.* 103.
		Cromwel's Con spiracy. TC.	[1660.]

Rogers and Ley, 1656.	Archer, 1656.	Kirkman, 1661 and 1671.	REMARKS.
Cruell brother.	Cruell brother. T.	*Sir W. D'Avenant.* Cruel Brother. T.	1630. *Pl.* 28.
	Cruel debtor. T.	Cruel Debtor.	William Wager. *Pl.* 116.
		Sir W. D'Avenant. Cruelty of the Spaniards in Peru. M. 1661] The	1658. *Mq.* 6
Cunning Lovers.	Cunning lovers. C.	*Alex. Brome.* Cunning Lover. C. 1661] lovers.	*The Cunning Lovers.* 1654. *Pl.* 13.
	Cupid and Death. M. *James Shirly.*	*James Shirley.* Cupid & Death. M.	1653. *Mq.* 24.
Cupids Revenge. *Beoment Flet.*	Cupids revenge. T.	*John Fletcher.* Cupids Revenge. C. 1661] T.	1615. *Pl.* 5.
Cupids whirligig.	Cupid's whirlygigg. C.	Cupids Whirligigg. C.	Edward Sharpham. The initials E. S. appear at the end of the dedication. *Pl.* 104.
		Webster & Rowly. Cure for a Cuckold. C. 1661] *omits* C.	In 'Two New Plays,' 1661. *Pl.* 117.
Custome of the country.	Custom of the country. C.	*John Fletcher.* Custome of the Countrey. C.	In folio 1647. *Pl.* 3.
Gardian, *Cowly.*	Guardian. C. *Abraham Cowly.*	*Abr. Cowley.* Guardian. C. *Abr. Cowley.* Cutter of Colemanstreet. C.	(*The Guardian.* 1650.) *Cutter of Coleman Street.* 1663. *Pl.* 24.
Cincbiline, *Shakspear.*	Cymbelona. T.	*Will. Shakespear.* Cymbeline. T.	In folio 1623. *Pl.* 94.

Rogers and Ley, 1656.	*Archer,* 1656.	*Kirkman,* 1661 *and* 1671.	REMARKS.
Cynthius Revenge.	Cynthia's revenge. T.	*John Swallow.* Cynthia's Revenge. T.	John Stephens. With dedication signed J. S. 1613, and another issue 'Written by John Stephens' 1613. *Pl.* 111. The ascription in Kirkman's list is important; see Halliwell & Fleay *ad. loc.*
Damsell, *Brome.*	Damoiselle. C. *Richard Broome.*	*Rich. Brome.* Damoyselle. C.	In 'Five new Plays,' 1653. *Pl.* 13.
Damon and Phithias.	Damon and Pithias. T.	Damon and Pythias. H.	1571. *Pl.* 36.
Darius Tragedy.	Daraia. T. *William Alexander.*	*Lord Sterling.* Darius. T.	William Alexander, E. of Stirling. 1603. *Pl.* 1.
Darius history.	Darus storie. H.	Darius story. I.	*Story of King Darius.* 1565. *Pl.* 123.
	Robert E. of Huntingtons death. H.	*Tho. Heywood.* Robert E. of Huntingdon's death. H.	*Anthony Munday. The death of Robert, E. of H.* 1601. *Pl.* 81. On the authority of Henslowe's diary.
		Rob. Baron. Deorum Dona. M.	[1647].
Favorite.	Favorite. C. *Lodowick Carlisle.*	*Lod. Carlile.* Deserving Favourite. TC.	1629. *Pl.* 16.
	Destruction of Jerusalem. M. *Thomas Legge.*	Destruction of Jerusalem.	Not known to have been printed.
Devils an asse. *B. J.*	Divel is an asse. C. *Ben. Johnson.*	*Ben. Johnson.* Devil is an Asse. C.	In Vol. II of folio 1640 (1631). *Pl.* 55.
Devills charter, or the life of Pope Alexander.	Divels charter. C. *Barnaby Barnes.*	*Barnaby Barnes.* Devils Charter. T. 1661] The	1607. *Pl.* 3.

Rogers and Ley, 1656.	*Archer,* 1656.	*Kirkman,* 1661 *and* 1671.	REMARKS.
Devils Law case.	Divels law-case. C. *Iohn Webster.*	*John Webster.* De-vils Law-case. TC.	1623. *Pl.* 118.
Dido Queen of Car-thage.	Dido Queen of Car-thage. T. *Christ. Marlow.*	*Marloe & Nash.* Dido Queen of Carthage. T.	1594. *Pl.* 67.
Discontented Col-lonel.	Brennerault. T. *John Suckling.* Discontented Col-onel. C. *John Suckling.*	*Sr. John Suckling.* Brenoralt. T.	*The Discontented Colonel.* n.d. (*Brennoralt.* In col. eds., 1646). *Pl.* 113, 112.
Disobedient childe.	Disobedient childe. C.	*Tho. Ingeland.* Dis-obedient Child. I.	n.d. *Pl.* 54.
Distracted State.	Distracted state. T. *John Tatham.*	*John Tateham.* Dis-tracted State. T.	1651. *Pl.* 114.
		1661 *only*] Don Quixot, or the Knight of the ill-favoured counten-ance. C.	'The History of Donquixiot, or the Knight of the ill-favoured face, a comedy' advertised at the end of Edward Phillips' *New World of English Words,* 1658, and of *Wit and Drollery,* 1661, as being in the press. Not now known. (Halliwell.)
Double Marriage.	Double marriage. C. *Iohn Fletcher.*	*John Fletcher.* Dou-ble Marriage. C.	In folio 1647. *Pl.* 3.
Doubtfull heire.	Doubtful heir. C. *James Shirly.*	*James Shirley.* Doubt-ful Heir. TC.	In 'Six new Plays,' 1653 *Pl.* 106.
Robert Earl of Hunt-ingtons downfall.	Robert E. of Hunt-ingtons downfall. H.	*Tho. Heywood.* Rob-ert E. of Hunting-don's downfal. H.	* Anthony Munday. *The Downfall of Robert, E. of H.* 1601. *Pl.* 81. On the autho-rity of Henslowe's diary.
		Sir W. D'Avenant. Drake's History, 1st. part. M.	*Sir Francis Drake.* 1659. *Mq.* 6.

Rogers and Ley, 1656.	Archer, 1656.	Kirkman, 1661 and 1671.	REMARKS.
Dutches of Malfie.	Dutchess of Malfy. T. *John Webster.*	*John Webster.* Dutchess of Malfy. T.	1623. *Pl.* 118.
Duke of Millaine.	Duke of Milain. T. *Phil. Massinger.*	*Phil. Massenger.* Duke of Millain. T.	1623. *Pl.* 73.
Dukes Mistresse. *Sherly.*	Dukes mistress. M. *Iames Shirly.*	*James Shirley.* Dukes Mistress. TC.	1638. *Pl.* 108.
Dumb Knight.	Dumbe Knight. C. *Lewis Machen.*	*Lewis Machin.* Dumb Knight. C.	Gervas Markham (preface signed Lewes Machin). 1608. *Pl.* 66.
Dutch curtizan, *Marston.*	Dutch curtisan. C. *John Marston.*	*John Marston.* Dutch Courtezan. C.	1605. *Pl.* 71.
Eastward ho. *B. J.*	Eastward ho. C. *George Chapman.*	*Chapman Johnson.* Eastward hoe. C.	George Chapman, Ben Ionson and John Marston. 1605. *Pl.* 19.
Edward I. *Long. Shanks.*	Edward first, Longshanks. T.	*Geo. Peele.* Edward the 1st. H.	1593. *Pl.* 84.
Edward 2. *Shakspear.*	Edward Second. T.	*Chr. Marloe.* Edward the 2d. T.	1594. *Pl.* 67.
Edward 3. *Shakspear.*	Edward Third. T.	*Edward* the 3d. H.	1596. *Pl.* 127.
Edward 4. *Shakspear.*	Edward Fourth, 2 parts. T.	*Tho. Heywood.* Edward the 4th. 1st part. C. *Tho. Heywood.* Edward the 4th. 2d. Part. 1661] *omits author's name in both cases.*	* 1600. *Pl.* 48. The ascription is doubtful.
Elder Brother, *Fletcher.*	Elder brother. C. *John Fletcher.*	*John Fletcher.* Elder Brother. C.	1637. *Pl.* 9.

Rogers and Ley, 1656.	*Archer,* 1656.	*Kirkman,* 1661 *and* 1671.	REMARKS.
	Electra sophoples (*sic*) T.	*C. W.* Electra of Sophocles. T.	[Christoper Wase. 1649].
		*Lord Digby. Elvira. C.	[**Elvira, or the Worst not always true.* 1667.]
Emperor East, *Messenger.*	Emperor of the East. C. *Philip Massinger.*	*Phil. Massenger.* Emperor of the East. C.	1632. *Pl.* 73.
		Sir Will. Lower. Enchanted Lovers. P. 1661] The	1658. *Pl.* 63.
Eudimion [*sic.*]	Endimion, or the man in the moon. C. *John Lilly.*	*John Lilly.* Endimion. C.	1591. *Pl.* 65.
	English Arcadia. C.		No doubt the *English Arcadia* by Gervase Markham, two parts, 1607 and 1613. It is, however, non-dramatic.
Woman will have her will.	Woman have her will. C.	Woman will have her will. C.	*William Haughton. Englishmen for my money* 1616. *A Woman* &c. 1631 *Pl.* 45. On the authority of Henslowe's Diary.
		Richard Brome. English Moor, or the Mock-marriage. C. 1661] The	In 'Five new Plays,' 1659. *Pl.* 14.
		*English Princess. T.	[J. Caryl. 1667.]
		*Tho. Thompson. English Rogue. C.	[1668.]

ı

Rogers and Ley, 1656.	*Archer,* 1656.	*Kirkman,* 1661 and 1671.	REMARKS.
English traveller. *Heywood.*	English traveller. C. *Tohmas* [sic] *Heywood.*	*Tho. Heywood.* English Traveller. C.	1633. *Pl.* 52.
Enough as good as a feast.	Enough as good as a feast. C.	Enough's as good as a Feast.	Not otherwise known.
Silent Woman. *Johnson.*	Silent woman. C. *Ben. Johnson.*	*Ben. Johnson.* Silent Woman. C.	*Epicœne.* 1620. *The S.W.* In folio 1616. *Pl.* 58 & 55.
		* *Rich. Flecknoe.* Erminia. TC.	[1661.]
	Eunuch in Terence. C. *Tho. Newman.*		With the *Andria.* 1627. *Pl.* 83.
Eunuchus [sic] terence.	Eunuchs in Terence. C. *Rich. Bernard.*	*Bernard.* Eunuchus in Terence. C.	*Richard Bernard.* In 'Terence in English,' 1598. *Pl.* 12.
		John Dreyden. Evening Love, or the Mock-Astrologer. C.	[*An Evening's Love, or the Mock Astrologer.* 1671].
Every man in his humor.	Every man in his humor. C. *Ben. Johnson.*	*Ben. Johnson.* Every Man in his humour. C.	1601. *Pl.* 56.
Every man out of his humor.	Every man out of his humor. C. *Ben. Johnson.*	*Ben. Johnson.* Every man out of his humour. C.	1600. *Pl.* 56.
Every woman in her humor.	Every woman in her humor. C. *Ben. Johnson.*	Every Woman in her humour. C	1609. *Pl.* 135.
Example, *Sherly.*	Example. C. *Iames Shirley.*	*James Shirley.* Example. 1661] C.	1637. *Pl.* 108.
	Extravagant shepherd. C. *Thomas Goffe.*	*T.R.* Extravagant Shepherd. C.	[1654.]

Rogers and Ley, 1656.	Archer, 1656.	Kirkman, 1661 and 1671.	REMARKS.
Millers Daughter of Manchester.	Faire Em, C. Millers daughter of Manchester. C.	Fair *Em.* C.	*Fair Em, the Miller's D. of M.* 1631. *Pl.* 137.
	Faire maid of Bristow. C.	Fair Maid of Bristol. 1661.] Bristow.	1605. *Pl.* 132.
	Faire maid of Exchange. C.	*Tho. Heywood.* Fair Maid of the Exchange. C. 1661] *omits the author's name.*	*1607. *Pl.* 50. The ascription lacks authority.
	Fair maid of the Inne. C. *John Fletcher.*	*John Fletcher.* Fair Maid of the Inne. C.	In folio 1647. *Pl.* 3.
Fair maid of the west.	Fair maid of the West. C. *Thomas Haywood.*	*Tho. Heywood.* Fair Maid of the West, 1st. part. C. *Tho. Heywood.* Fair Maid of the West, 2d. part. C.	1631. *Pl.* 52.
Faire quarrel.	Fair quarrel. C. *Thomas Midelton.*	*Midleton & Rowly.* Fair Quarrel. TC.	1617. *Pl.* 78.
Faithfull Shepheardesse.	Faithfull Shepheardesse. C. *John Dymmocke.*	*John Fletcher.* Faithful Shepherdess. P.	1629. *Pl.* 9. For name in Archer's list *see Pastor Fido.*
		Geo. Gerbier D'ouvilly. False Favourite disgrac'd. TC.	[1657.]
False one. *F. Beament.*	False one. C. *John Fletcher.*	*John Fletcher* False one. T.	In folio 1647. *Pl.* 3.
Family of Love.	Family of love. C. *Thomas Middlton* [sic.]	*Tho. Midleton* Family of Love. C.	* 1608. *Pl.* 77.

Rogers and Ley, 1656.	*Archer,* 1656.	*Kirkman,* 1661 *and* 1671.	REMARKS.
	Henry the Fifth, with the battel of Agincourt. C.	Henry the 5th. with the Battel of Agen-Court. H.	*The Famous Victories of &c.* 1598. *Pl.* 127.
Fancies. *J. Ford.*	Fancies. C.	*John Ford.* Fancies. C.	*The Fancies Chaste and Noble.* 1638. *Pl.* 38.
		Tho. Jordain. Fancies Festivals. M.	[1657.]
	Fatall Contract. C.	*Will. Hemings.* Fatal contract. T.	1653. *Pl.* 46.
Fatall Dowry.	Fatall Dowery. C. *Philip Massenger.*	*Phil. Massinger.* Fatal Dowry. T.	Philip Massinger & Nathaniel Field. 1632. *Pl.* 74.
Faustus life and death.	Doctor Faustus. H.	*Chr. Marloe.* Doctor Faustus. T.	1604. *Pl.* 68.
		*Feigned Astrologer. C	[Anon. 1668.]
Gorbuduck, or Ferex and Procex. [*sic.*]	{ Ferex and Porex. C. Gorbodne [*sic*]. C.	*Tho. Norton.* Ferex and Porex. T.	Thomas Norton & Thomas Sackville. (*Gorboduc* 1565) *F. & P.* n.d. *Pl.* 83.
Fidele and fortunio.	Fidele and Fortunata. C.	Fidele and Fortunatus. 1661] Fortunata.	[*The Two Italian Gentlemen*]. Anthony Munday. n.d. *Pl.* 81. *F. and F.* appears from this to have been the proper title.
	Scirio and Phillis. P.	*J.S.* Phillis of Scyros. P.	*Filli di Sciro, or Phillis of Scyros.* 1655. *Pl.* 137.
Fine compagnion, *Shakerly, Me:*	Fine Companion. C. *Shakerly Mermyon.*	*Shak. Marmion.* Fine companion. C.	1633. *Pl.* 69.
Fleere sharpham.	Fleire. C. *Edward Sharpham.*	Fleire. C.	1607. *Pl.* 105.
	Floating Island. C.	*Will. Strode.* Floating Island. C.	1655. *Pl.* 112.

Rogers and Ley, 1656.	*Archer,* 1656.	*Kirkman,* 1661 *and* 1671.	REMARKS.
		* *Rhodes.* Flora's Fagaries. C.	[Richard Rhodes. 1670.]
		Flowers. M.	*The Masque of Flowers.* 1614. *Mq.* 27.
		Lod. Carlile. Fool would be a Favourite, or the discreet Lover. TC. 1661] The.	In 'Two new Plays.' 1657. *Pl.* 16.
		* *Astrea Bien.* Forced Marriage, or the jealous Bridegroom. TC.	[Alphra Behn. 1671.]
	Fortunate Isles. M.	*Ben. Johnson.* Fortunate Isles. M.	n.d. *Mq.* 15.
	Fortunate Isles. C.		Unless this is a duplicate entry, I cannot identify it.
Fortune both by Land and Sea.	Fortune by land and sea. C.	*Tho. Heywood.* Fortune by Land and Sea. C.	Thomas Heywood & William Rowley. 1655. *Pl.* 54.
Cynthius Revels, *Fountaine.*	Cynthius Revels. T. *Ben Johnson.*	*Ben. Johnson.* Cynthia's Revels. C.	(*The Fountain of Self-Love.* 1601.) *Cynthia's Revells.* In folio 1616. *Pl.* 57 & 55.
Four Pees.	Four pees. C.	* *John Heywood.* Four PP. I.	1569. *Pl.* 48.
Four Plays in one, *B. F.*	Foure plays in one. C. *John Fletcher.*	*John Fletcher.* Four Playes in One. C.	In folio 1647. *Pl.* 3.
Four London Prentices, *Heyw:*	Foure London prentises. T. *Thomas Haywood.*	*Tho. Heywood.* Four London Prentices. H.	*The four Prentices of London.* 1615. *Pl.* 52.
Freewill.	Free will. C. *Henry Cheeke.*	Free-will. T.	Henry Cheeke. n.d. *Pl.* 22.

Rogers and Ley, 1656.	*Archer,* 1656.	*Kirkman,* 1661 *and* 1671.	REMARKS.
Friar Bacon, *Green.*	Fryer bacon. H.	*Robert Green.* Frier Bacon. C.	*Friar Bacon & Friar Bungay.* 1594. *Pl.* 43.
Fulgius and Lucrell.	Fulgius and Lucrell. C.	Fulgius & Lucrel.	Chetwood, in his *British Theatre,* gives "Fulgius and Lucrette, a pastoral, from the Italian, 1676," but no authority attaches to the statement.
Galatea, *Lilly.*	Galatea. C. *John Lilly.*	*John Lilly.* Galla-thea. C.	1592. *Pl.* 65.
Game at Chesse.	Game at chesse C. *Thomas Middleton.*	*Tho. Midleton.* Game at Chess. C.	1625. *Pl.* 79.
Gamester, *Sherly.*	Gamester. C. *Iames Shirly.*	*James Shirley.* Gamester. C.	1637. *Pl.* 108.
Gammer Gurtons needle.	Gammer Gurtons needle. C.	*Mr. S. Mr. of Art.* Gammer Gurtons Needle. C.	Iohn Still. 1575. *Pl.* 112.
	Gentleman of Ve-nice. H. *Iames Shirley.*	*James Shirley.* Gen-tleman of Venice. TC.	1655. *Pl.* 110.
	Gentleman Usher. C. *Georg Chap-man.*	*George Chapman.* Gentleman Usher. 1661] The	1606. *Pl.* 19.
		John Heywood. Play of Gentleness & Nobility. 1st. part. I. 1661] A Play of... Nobility &c. the *John Heywood.* Play of Gentleness & Nobility &c. 2d. part. I. 1661] A Play ... the 2d part.	*n.d. *Pl.* 48.

Rogers and Ley, 1656.	*Archer,* 1656.	*Kirkman,* 1661 *and* 1671.	REMARKS.
Pinder of Wakefield.	George a Green. C. Pinner of Wakefild. C.	Pinner of Wuke-field. C. 1661] The Pinner of Wakefield.	*George-a-Greene, the Pinner of Wakefield.* 1599. *Pl.* 129.
Ghost, or the woman wears the breeches.	Ghost. C.	Ghost. C.	1653. *Pl.* 137.
Glasse of Government.	Glasse of govern-ment. I. *Georg Gascoyne.*	*Geo. Gascoign.* Glass of Government. TC. 1661] The	1575. *Pl.* 40.
Goblins sucklin.	Gobline. C. *Iohn Sucklinge.*	*Sir John Suckling.* Goblins. C.	In col. ed. 1646. *Pl.* 112.
Golden age, *Hey-wood.*	Golden Age. C. *Thomas Haywood.*	*Tho. Heywood.* Golden Age. H.	1611. *Pl.* 51.
		*Ben. Johnson. Golden Age restored. M.	In 1616 folio. *Mq.* 12.
Giles Goosecap.	Gyles Goose-cap. C.	Gyles Goose cap. C.	*Sir Giles Goosecap.* 1606. *Pl.* 132.
Gratefull servant, *Sherly.*	Gratefull servant. C. *James Shirly.*	*James Shirley.* Grateful Servant. C.	1630. *Pl.* 106.
Masque of the gen-tlemen of Grays In.	Mask at Graies-Inn. M.	*John Fletcher.* Masque of Grays Inne Gent. M.	*Inner Temple & Gray's Inn Masque* Francis Beau-mont. n.d. *Mq.* 1.
Great Duke of Florence.	Duke of Florence. T.	*Phil. Massenger.* Great Duke of Florence. C.	1636. *Pl.* 74.
		*Sr. Rob. Howard The Great Fa-vourite, or, the Duke of Lerma. T.	[1668.] Added in Adver-tisement at end of list.

Rogers and Ley, 1656.	*Archer,* 1656.	*Kirkman,* 1661 *and* 1671.	REMARKS.
Greens tu quoque cookt.	Greens tu quoque. C. *Iohn Cooke.*	*John Cooke.* Green's tu quoque. C.	1614. *Pl.* 23.
		*J.T. Grim the Collier of Croyden. C.	* William Haughton ('by I.T.') In *Gratiæ Theatrales,* 1662. *Pl.* 46. On the authority of Henslowe's Diary.
		Rob. Baron. Gripus & Hegio. P.	[1647.]
	Guardian. C. *Phil. Massinger.*	*Phil. Massenger.* Guardian. C.	In 'Three new Plays,' 1655. *Pl.* 72.
Guise, *Marstone.*	Guise. C. *Iohn Webster.*	Guise. T. 1661] *omits* T.	There was a play of this name by Webster, which is not, however, known to have been printed. The *Massacre at Paris* was also sometimes known by this name.
		* *B. J.* Guy of Warwick. T.	[*Guy, Earl of Warwick.* 1661. Probably the initials were intended to suggest that the play was by Jonson.]
Hamlet Prince of Denmark.	Hamblet prince of den. T. *Will. Shakespeare.*	*Will. Shakespear.* Hamlet. T.	1603. *Pl.* 100.
Haniball and Sc[i]pio.	Hanniball and Scipio. C. *Tho. Nabbs.*	*Tho. Nabs.* Hannibal & Scipio. T.	1637. *Pl.* 82.
		Ben. Johnson. Masque at my Lord Hayes House. M.	In Vol. II of folio 1640. *Mq.* 12.
		Bearnard. Heauton. in Ter. C. 1661] Bernard.	*Heautontimoroumenos.* Richard Bernard. In *Terence in English.* 1598. *Pl.* 12.

Rogers and Ley, 1656.	*Archer,* 1656.	*Kirkman,* 1661 *and* 1671.	REMARKS.
Hector of Germany.	{ Hector of Germany. C. Palsgrave. T.	*W. S.* Hector of Germany. H. 1661] *W. Smith.*	*The Hector of Germany, or The Palsgrave.* W[entworth?]. Smith. 1615. *Pl.* III.
	Hectors. C.	Hectors, or false challenge. C.	[1656.]
Heire, *May.*	Heir. C. *Tho. May.*	*Tho. May.* Heire. TC.	1622. *Pl.* 75.
		＊ J. D. Hels higher court of Justice. I.	[1661.]
Henry the 4. both parts. *Shakspear.*	Henry Fourth, both parts. H. *Will. Shakespeare.*	| *Will. Shakespear.* Henry the 4th. 1st. part. H. | *Will. Shakespear.* Henry the 4th. 2d. part. H.	Pt. I. 1598. Pt. II. 1600. *Pl.* 97 & 98.
Henry 5. *Shakspear.*	Henry Fifth. H. *Will. Shakespeare.*	*Will. Shakespear.* Henry the 5th. H.	1600. *Pl.* 98.
		＊ Earl of Orrery. Henry the 5th. H.	[1669.]
Henry 6 three parts. *Shakspear.*	Henry Sixth. 3 parts. H. *Will. Shakespeare.*	| *Will. Shakespear.* Henry the 6th. 1st. part. H. | *Will. Shakespear.* Henry the 6th. 2d. part. H. | *Will. Shakespear.* Henry the 6th. 3d. part. H.	In folio 1623. *Pl.* 94.
Hen[r]y 8. *Shakspear.*	Henry Eight. H. *Will. Shakespeare.*	*Will. Shakespear.* Henry the 8th. H.	In folio 1623. *Pl.* 94.
		＊ Lod. Carlile. Heraclius Emperour of the East. T.	1664. *Pl.* 17.

Rogers and Ley, 1656.	*Archer,* 1656.	*Kirkman,* 1661 and 1671.	REMARKS.
Hercules furiens.	Hercules furious. I.	*Jasper Heywood.* Hercules furiens. T.	From Seneca. 1561. *Pl.* 93.
Hercules Orteous.	Hercules Orteus. I.	*John Studley.* Hercules Oetus. T.	*Hercules Œtæus.* In col. Seneca. 1581. *Pl.* 92.
		*Sir Rob. Stapleton. Hero & Leander. T.	[1669.]
Herod and Antipater.	Herod Antipater. C. *George Markham.*	*Markham and Sampson.* Herod and Antipater T.	1622. *Pl.* 66.
		*R. Head. Hic & Ubique. C.	[1663.]
Dick Scorner.	Dick Scorner. C.	Dick Scorner.	*Hickescorner.* n.d. *Pl.* 139.
Hide park.	Hide Parke. C. *James Shirly.*	*James Shirley.* Hide Park. C.	1637. *Pl.* 108.
		John Studley. Hyppolitus. T.	In col. Seneca 1581. *Pl.* 92.
Hipolitus.	Hippolitus Seneca. T. *Edmund Prestwich.*	*Edm. Prestwith* Hyppolitus. T.	[1651.]
Player whipt.	{Histriomastix. C. {Player whipt. C.	Histriomastix. C.	1610. *Pl.* 135.
Hofmans Tragedy.	Hoffman. T. *William Shakespeare.*	*Hoffman. T.	*Henry Chettle. 1631. *Pl.* 22. On the authority of Henslowe's diary.
Hog hath lost his Pearl.	Hog hath lost his pearle. C. *Robt. Taylor.*	*Rob. Taylor.* Hog hath lost his Pearl. C.	1614. *Pl.* 113.

Rogers and Ley, 1656.	Archer, 1656.	Kirkman, 1661 and 1671.	REMARKS.
Hollands Leagure.	Holands Leaguer. H. *Shakerly Marmion.*	*Shak. Marmion.* Hollands Leaguer. C.	1632. *Pl.* 69.
	Hollander. C. *Henry Glapthorn.*	*Henry Glapthorn.* Hollander. C.	1640. *Pl.* 41.
Honest Lawyer.	Honest Lawyer. C.	*S. S.* Honest Lawyer. C. 1661] The	1616. *Pl.* 135.
Honest mans fortune.	Honest mans fortune. C.	*John Fletcher.* Honest mans fortune. C.	In folio 1647. *Pl.* 3.
Honest whore both parts.	Honest, both parts. C. *Tho. Decker.*	*Tho. Decker.* Honest Whore, 1st. part. C. *Tho. Decker.* Honest Whore, 2d. part. C.	Pt. I. 1604. Pt. II. 1630. *Pl.* 33 & 34.
		James Shirley. Honoria and Mamon.	1659. *Pl.* 110.
		Ben. Johnson. Honour of Wales. M.	In Vol. II of folio 1640. *Mq.* 12.
		*Mr. Rat. Phillips. Horace. T.	*Mrs. Kat. P.* In 'Poems' 1667. Act V by Sir John Denham. *Pl.* 35.
	Horatius. T. *Wil. Lower.*	*Sir W. Lower.* Horatius. T.	1656. *Pl.* 63.
How to choose a good wife from a bad.	Choice, a good wife from a bad. C.	How to choose a good wife from a bad. TC.	*How a man may choose,* &c. 1602. *Pl.* 131.
Humor out of breath, *Chapman.*	Humor out of breath. C. *John Doy.*	*John Day.* Humour out of breath. C.	1608. *Pl.* 31.

Rogers and Ley, 1656.	*Archer,* 1656.	*Kirkman,* 1661 *and* 1671.	REMARKS.
Humerous Courtier, *Sherly*.	Humerous Courtier. C. *James Shirly*.	*James Shirley*. Humorous Courtier. C.	1640. *Pl.* 109.
	Humerous dayes mirth. C. *Gorge Chapman*.	*Geo. Chapman*. Humorous dayes mirth. C.	1599. *Pl.* 19.
Humerous Live-tenant.	Humerous Live-tenant. C. *John Fletcher*.	*John Fletcher*. Humorous Lieut-enant. C.	In folio 1647. *Pl.* 3.
Hymens triumph.	Hymens Triumph. M. *Samuel Daniel*.	*Sam. Daniel*. Hy-mens Triumph. P.	1615. *Pl.* 27.
	Hymeniæ. M.	**Ben Johnson*. Hy-menæ. M.	1606. *Mq.* 14.
If this be not a good Play the Devils in't.	If this be not a good play the devils in't. C. *Tho. Decker*.	*Tho. Decker*. If this be'nt a good Play, the Devil's in't. C.	*If it be not good, the Devil is in it*. 1612. *Pl.* 34.
If you know not me you know no body.	Elisabeth 1. 2. part. T.	*Tho. Heywood*. Elizabeth's trou-bles, 1st. part. *Tho. Heywood*. Eli-zabeth's troubles, 2d. part. 1661] H *in both cases.*	**If you know not me you know nobody, or the Troubles of Queen Elizabeth*. Pt. I. 1605. Pt. II. 1606. *Pl.* 49.
	Ignoramus. C.	**R.C.* Ignoramus. C.	[The English translation by Robert Codrington of George Ruggle's Latin comedy of *Ignoramus* ap-peared in 1662. The entry in Archer's list must there-fore refer to the Latin play which appeared in 1630.]
	Impatient Grissell. C.		No such piece is known.

Rogers and Ley, 1656.	*Archer,* 1656.	*Kirkman,* 1661 *and* 1671.	REMARKS.
Impatient potency.	Impatient Poverty. C.	Impatient poverty.	1560. *Pl.* 122.
Imperiale, *Freeman.*	Imperiall. T.	*Sr. Ralph Freeman.* Imperiale. T.	1639. *Pl.* 39.
		*Imperiale, in Folio. T.	[Presumably *The Imperial Tragedy.* Sir William Killigrew. F° 1669.]
Imposter, *Sherly.*	Imposter. C. *Iames Shirly.*	*James Shirley.* Imposture. TC	In 'Six new Plays,' 1653. *Pl.* 106.
		John Dreyden. Indian Emperor. T.	[1667.]
		Sir Rob. Howard. Indian queen. T.	[Sir Robert Howard and John Dryden. In the former's 'Four New Plays,' 1665.]
Insatiat Countesse.	Insatiate Countess. C. *John Marston.*	*John Marston.* Insatiate Countess. T.	1613. *Pl.* 71.
		Tho. Midleton. Inner Temple Masque. M. 1661] The	1619. *Mq.* 17.
		Geo. Chapman. Temple. M. *George Chapman.* Masque of the middle Temple, & Lincolns Inn. M. 1661.] The Mask	*Inns of Court Masque.* n.d. *Mq.* 3.
		Ben. Johnson. Irish Masque. M.	In folio 1616. *Mq.* 12.

Rogers and Ley, 1656.	Archer, 1656.	Kirkman, 1661 and 1671.	REMARKS.
Iron age both parts.	Iron age, both parts. C. *Tho. Decker.*	*Tho. Heywood.* Iron Age First part. H. *Tho. Heywood.* Iron Age, Second part. H.	Pt. I. 1632. Pt. II. 1632. *Pl.* 52.
Island Princes, *BF.*	Island princess. C. *John Fletcher.*	*John Fletcher.* Island Princess. C.	In folio 1647. *Pl.* 3.
Isle of Gulls.	Isle of gall. H. *Pow. Day.*	*John Day.* Isle of Guls. C. 1661] *omits* C.	1606. *Pl.* 31.
Jack drums entertainment.	Iack drums entertainement.	Jack Drums Entertainment. C. 1661] T.	1601. *Pl.* 130.
Jack jugler.	Iack jugler. C.	Jack Jugler	n.d. *Pl.* 139.
Jack Straws life and death.	Iack Strawes life and death. H.	Jack Straw's life and death. H.	1593. *Pl.* 125.
Jacob and Esau.	Iacob and Esau. I.	Jacob and Esau. C.	1568. *Pl.* 123.
Scotch Hist. *James* the 4.	Scotch historie. H.	James the 4th. H.	(*The Scottish History of* *Iames the fourth.* Robert Greene. 1598. *Pl.* 44.
Jealous lovers, *Randolph.*	Iealous lovers. C. *Tho. Randolph.*	*Tho. Randal.* Jealous Lovers. C. 1661] *Randoll.*	Thomas Randolph. 1632. *Pl.* 88.
		Jeronimo. See *Spanish Tragedy*	
Jew of Malta.	Jew of Malta. H. *Christ. Marlow.*	*Chr. Marloe.* Jew of Malta. TC. 1661] T.	1633. *Pl.* 69.
		*Will. Hemings. Jews Tragedy. T.	1662. *Pl.* 47.

Rogers and Ley, 1656.	*Archer,* 1656.	*Kirkman,* 1661 *and* 1671.	REMARKS.
Jocasta. *Gascoine.*	Iorasta [*sic*]. H.	*Geo. Gascoign.* Jocasta. T.	In col. ed. 1575. *Pl.* 39.
		John Heywood. Play between Johan Johan the husband, Tib his Wife, &c. I. 1661] A	*1533. *Pl.* 47.
	John K. of England. H.	*Will. Shakespear.* John King of England. H.	*King John.* In folio 1623. *Pl.* 94.
John King of England both parts.	Iohn K. of England, both parts. *Will. Shakespeare.*	{*Will. Shakespear.* John K. of England, 1st. part. H. *Will. Shakespear.* John K. of England, 2d. part. H.	*The Troublesome Reign of Iohn King of England.* Author unknown. 1591 anon. 1611 'by W. Sh.' 1622 'by W. Shakespeare.' *Pl.* 124.
King John and Matilda.	K. Iohn and Matilda. T.	*Rob. Davenport.* John & Matilda. T.	1655. *Pl.* 30.
	Iohn Evangelist. I.	John Evangelist.	Neither Langbaine nor any of his followers had seen the piece. The *Biographia Dramatica* gives the date 1566, which, however, appears to be an invention of Chetwood's.
	Iosephs afflictions. I.	Josephs afflictions.	The *Biographia Dramatica* suggests that it may either be a mistake for *Iob's Afflictions*, a play ascribed by Wood to Ralph Radcliff, but not at present known, or else may refer to William Forrest's poem *The tragedious troubles of the most chast and innocent Joseph.*

Rogers and Ley, 1656.	*Archer,* 1656.	*Kirkman,* 1661 *and* 1671.	REMARKS.
Joviall Crew, or merry beggers.	Iovial crew. C. *Rich. Brome.*	*Rich. Brome.* Jovial crew.† C.	1652, *Pl.* 15.
Jovall Crew, *Shepheard.*		*Jovial crew, or the Devil turn'd Ranter. I.	[1651.]
Julia and Agripina. Agripina.	Agrippina. T. *Thomas May.*	*Tho. May.* Agrippina. T.	*Julia Agrippina.* 1639. *Pl.* 76.
Julius Cæsar, *Sterling.* Cæsars Tragedy, *Sterlin.*	Cæsar. T. *William Alexander.*	*Lord Sterling.* Julius Cæsar. T.	William Alexander, E. of Stirling. In the *Monarchic Tragedies,* 1607. *Pl.* 1.
Julius Cæsar, *Shakspear.*	Julius Cæsar. T. *Will. Shakespeare.*	*Will. Shakespear.* Julius Cæsar. T.	In folio 1623. *Pl.* 94.
Just generall, *Cosmo Muche.*	Iust generall. T. *Cosmo Manuche.*	*Cosmo Manuch.* Just General. T.	[Cosmo Manuche. 1652]
Just Italian, *Davenant.*	Just Italian. C. *Will. Davenant.*	*Sir W. D'Avenant.* Just Italian. TC.	1630. *Pl.* 28.
King and no King, *Fletcher.*	King and no King. C. *John Fletcher.*	*John Fletcher.* King and no King. C.	1619. *Pl.* 7.
Knack to know a knave.	Knack to know a knave. C.	Knack to know a Knave. C.	1594. *Pl.* 126.
Knack to know an honest man.	Knack to know an honest man. C.	Knack to know an honest man. C.	1596. *Pl.* 127.
	Knave in Graine. C.	*J. D.* Knave in grain. C.	1640. *Pl.* 137.
		* Knavery in all trades. C.	[1664. Hazlitt ascribes it to Tatham without, however, giving any reason.]

† In 1661 the letters denoting the nature of the play have slipped down at this point, causing some confusion I have followed the evident intention of 1661, but in 1671 some mistakes crept in from the disorder of the earlier edition. See *Jew of Malta.*

Rogers and Ley, 1656.	*Archer,* 1656.	*Kirkman,* 1661 *and* 1671.	REMARKS.
	Knight of malta. H. *John Fletcher.*	*John Fletcher.* Knight of Malta. C.	In folio 1647. *Pl.* 3.
	Knight of pestell. C. *Iohn Fletcher.*	*John Fletcher.* Knight of the burning pestle. C.	1613. *Pl.* 4.
	Ladyes privilege. C. *Iames Shirly.*	*Hen. Glapthorn.* Ladies Priviledge. C.	1640. *Pl.* 41.
		Lady Almony. C.	1659. *Pl.* 137.
Lady errant.	Ladie errant. C. *William Cartwright.*	*W. Cartwright.* Lady Errant. TC.	In col. ed. 1651. *Pl.* 17.
	Ladies trial. C. *John Ford.*	*John Ford.* Ladies Tryal. C.	1639. *Pl.* 38.
Lady of pleasure.	Lady of pleasure. C. *Henry Glapthorn.*	*James Shirley.* Lady of Pleasure. C.	1637. *Pl.* 108.
Langartha, *Henry Burrel.*	Langartha. C.	Landagartha. TC.	*Landgartha.* Henry Burnell. 1641. *Pl.* 15.
Alarum for *London,* or the siege of *Antwerp.*	Alarum for London. T.	Alarum for London. H.	*A Larum for London.* 1602. *Pl.* 131.
Lanchashiere witches.	Lancaster witches. C.	*Heywood & Brome.* Lancaster Witches. C.	*The late Lancashire Witches.* 1634. *Pl.* 52.
Law tricks, or who would have thought it.	Law-tricks. C.	*John Day.* Law tricks, or who would have thought it. C. 1661] it?	1608. *Pl.* 31.
Laws of Candy.	Laws of Candy. C. *F.B. Iohn Fletcher.*	*John Fletcher.* Lawes of Candy. C.	In folio 1647. *Pl.* 3.

K

Rogers and Ley, 1656.	Archer, 1656.	Kirkman, 1661 and 1671.	REMARKS.
Leyre and his three daughters. *Shak:*		*Will. Shakespear.* Leir and his three Daughters. T.	*King Lear and his three Daughters.* 1608. *Pl.* 101.
		Leir and his three Daughters. H.	1605. *Pl.* 132.
Levelers.	Leveller levelled. C.	*Levellers Levell'd. I.	['Mercurius Pragmaticus, *i.e.*, Marchmont Nedham. 1647.]
Like to like quoth the Devil to the Collier.	Like for like. C.	*Ulpian Fulwel.* Like will to like, quoth the Devil. I.	1568. *Pl.* 39.
Lingua.	Lingua. C.	Lingua. C.	1607. *Pl.* 134.
Little French Lawyer.	Little French-lawyer. C. *F.B. Jo. F.*	*John Fletcher.* Little French Lawyer. C.	In folio 1647. *Pl.* 3.
Locrinus Tragedy.	Locrinus. C.	*Will. Shakespear.* Locrine Eldest Son of K. Brutus. T. 1661] *W.S.*	'By W. S.' Pseudo-Shak. 1595. *Pl.* 102.
		Rob. Gomersal. Lod. Sforza. T.	1628. *Pl.* 43.
London or the harbor of health.			*Londini Sinus Salutis.* Thomas Heywood. 1635. *Mq.* 10.
		* *Ben. Johnson.* Entertainments at King James's coronation. E.	*King James his Entertainment through London.* 1604. *Mq.* 13.
		London Chanticlers. C. 1661] The	1659. *Pl.* 138.
London Prodigall, *Shakspear.*	London prodigall. C. *Will. Shakespear.*	*Will. Shakespear.* London Prodigal. C.	'by W. S.' Pseudo-Shak. 1605. *Pl.* 103.

Rogers and Ley, 1656.	*Archer,* 1656.	*Kirkman,* 1661 and 1671.	REMARKS.
The longer thou livest, the more foole thou art.	The longer thou livest, the more fool thou art. C.	*W. Wayer.* The longer thou livest the more fool thou art. C.	William Wager. n.d. *Pl.* 116.
Look about you or run red cap.	Look about you. C.	Look about you, or, run Red Caps. C.	*Look about you.* 1600. *Pl.* 130.
Looking glas for London & England.	Looking-glasse for London. C.	*Jho. Lodge and Robert Green.* Looking-glass for London. H. 1661] A Looking-glasse for London, &c.	1594. *Pl.* 62.
Lost Lady.	Lost Ladie. C. *F. B. Jo. Fl.*	Lost Lady. TC.	*Sir William Berkeley. 1638. Pl. 12. On the authority of Anthony Wood.
		John Heywood. Play of Love. I. 1661] A.	1534. *Pl.* 143 & 48.
Loves cure of martiall madnesse.	Loves Cruelty or the Martials maide. C. *F. B. Jo. F.*	*John Fletcher.* Loves cure, or the martial Maid. C.	In folio 1647. *Pl.* 3.
Loves Cruelty, *Sherly.*	Loves cruelty. C. *F. B. Jo. F.*	*James Shirley.* Loves Cruelty. T.	1640. *Pl.* 109.
	Loves dominion. P.	Loves Dominion. P.	[Richard Flecknoe. 1654.]
		Rich. Flecknoe. Loves Kingdom. T.C.	[1664.]
Loves labor lost.	Loves labor lost. C. *Will. Shakespeare.*	*Will. Shakespear.* Loves labour lost. C.	1598. *Pl.* 98.
	Loves labor lost. C. *Will. Sampson.*		Presumably a duplicate entry of Shakespeare's play.

Rogers and Ley, 1656.	*Archer,* 1656.	*Kirkman,* 1661 *and* 1671.	REMARKS.
		* T. Ford. Loves Labyrinth. TC.	[1660.]
Loves metamorphosis.	Loves metamorphosis. C. *John Lilly.*	*John Lilly.* Loves Metamorphosis. C.	1601. *Pl.* 65.
Loves Mistresse, Heywood.	Loves Mistriss. M. *Thomas Haywood.*	*Tho. Heywood.* Loves Mistress. M.	*Love's Mistress, or the Queen's Masque.* 1636. *Pl.* 53.
Loves Pilgrimage *B.F:*	Loves Pilgrim. C. *E. B. Jo. Fl.*	*John Fletcher.* Loves Pilgrimage. C.	In folio 1647. *Pl.* 3.
Loves Riddle, *Lowly.*	Loves riddle. P. *Abraham Cowley.*	*Abra. Cowley.* Loves Riddle. P.	1638. *Pl.* 24.
Loves Sacrifice.	Loves Sacrifice. C. *John Ford.*	*John Ford.* Loves Sacrifice. T.	1633. *Pl.* 37.
	Loves triumph. .M.	*Ben. Johnson.* Loves Triumph. M.	1630. *Mq.* 15.
		W. Chamberlain. Loves Victory. C.	[1658.]
		Ben. Johnson. Loves Welcome. M.	In vol. II of folio 1640. *Mq.* 13.
		*Love Alamode. C.	[*Love à la Mode.* 1663.]
	Love and fortune. C.		(*The Rare Triumphs of*) *Love and Fortune.* 1589. *Pl.* 123.
Love and honour.	Love and honor. C. *Will. Davenant.*	*Sir W. D'Avenant.* Love & Honour. C.	1649. *Pl.* 28.
		Tho. Meriton. Love and War. T.	[1658.]

Rogers and Ley, 1656.	*Archer,* 1656.	*Kirkman,* 1661 *and* 1671.	REMARKS.
		John Tatham. Love crowns the end. TC.	In *Fancie's Theatre,* 1640. *Pl.* 114.
		* *Ben. Johnson.* Love freed from Ignorance. M.	In folio 1616. *Mq.* 12.
Love in an extasie.	Love in its extasie. C.	*Peaps.* Love in it's Extasie. P.	*1649. *Pl.* 84. The ascription originally rests upon Kirkman's authority.
David and Bathsheba.	David and Beersheba. T. *George Pele.*	*Geo. Peel.* David & Bathsabe. TC.	*The Love of King D. and fair B.* 1599. *Pl.* 85.
		* *Ben. Johnson.* Love restored. M.	In folio 1616. *Mq.* 12.
		Rich. Brome. Lovesick Court, or the ambitious Politick. C. 1661] The	In 'Five new Plays,' 1659. *Pl.* 14.
Love sick King, *Brewer.*	Love-sick King. C. *Thomas Bernard.*	*Ant. Brewer.* Lovesick King. TC.	1655. *Pl.* 143.
	Lovers, a mask. M.		*Lovers made Men.* Ben Jonson. 1617. *Mq.* 15.
Lovers melancholy.	Loves Melancholy. C. *John Foard.*	*John Ford.* Lovers Melancholy. T.	1629. *Pl.* 37.
Loves progresse.	Loves progresse. C. *F. B. Jo. F.*	*John Fletcher.* Lovers Progress. C.	In folio 1647. *Pl.* 3.
Loyall lovers, *Cosmo muche.*	Loial lovers. C. *Cosmo Manuche.*	*Cosmo Manuch.* Loyal Lovers. TC.	[Cosmo Manuche. 1652.]
Loyall subject.	Loial subject. C. *F. B. Jo. F.*	*John Fletcher.* Loyal Subject. C.	In folio 1647. *Pl.* 3.

Rogers and Ley, 1656.	Archer, 1656.	Kirkman, 1661 and 1671.	REMARKS.
		Luminalia. M.	1637. *Mq.* 28.
Lusty Juventus.	Lustie juventus. C.	*R. Wever.* Lusty Juventus. I.	n.d. *Pl.* 119.
		Chr. Marloe. Lusts Dominion, or the Lascivious Queen. T.	1657. *Pl.* 69.
Mackbeth, *Shakspear.*	Magbeth. T. *Will. Shakespeer.*	*Will. Shakespear.* Mackbeth. T.	In folio 1623. *Pl.* 94.
Mad couple well met, *Brome.*	Mad couple. C. *Richard Broome.*	*Rich. Brome.* Mad Couple well matcht. C.	In 'Five new Plays,' 1653. *Pl.* 13.
Mad lover, *Fletcher.*	Mad lover. C. *John Fletcher.*	*John Fletcher.* Mad Lover. C.	In folio 1647. *Pl.* 3.
Mad world my Masters.	Mad world my masters. C. *Thomas Middleton.*	*Tho. Midleton.* Mad World my Masters. C.	1608. *Pl.* 78.
Magnetick Lady.	Magnetick Lady. C.	*Ben. Johnson.* Magnetick Lady. C.	In Vol. II of folio 1640. *Pl.* 55.
{ Maids in the mil. { Maid in the mill.	Maid in the mil. C. *Will. Rouly.*	*John Fletcher.* Maid in the Mill. C.	In folio 1647. *Pl.* 3.
Maids of honour.	Maid of honour. C. *Phil. Massinger.*	*Phil. Massenger.* Maid of Honour. C.	1632. *Pl.* 74.
Maids metomorphosis.	Maids metamorphosis. C. *Iohn Lilly.*	*John Lilly.* Maids Metamorphosis. C.	Author unknown. 1600. *Pl.* 130.
Maids revenge, *Sherly.*	Maids revenge. T. *Iames Shirly.*	*James Shirley.* Maids Revenge. T.	1639. *Pl.* 109.
Maids Tragedy, *Fletcher.*	Maids Tragedy. T. *F.B. Jo. Fl.*	*John Fletcher.* Maids Tragedy. T.	1619. *Pl.* 6.

Rogers and Ley, 1656.	*Archer,* 1656.	*Kirkman,* 1661 *and* 1671.	REMARKS.
Maidenhead well lost, *Heywood.*	Maidenhead well lost. C. *Thomas Haywood.*	*Tho. Heywood.* Maiden head well lost. C.	1634. *Pl.* 53.
Male content, *Marstone.*	Male-content. C. *Iohn Marston.*	*John Marston.* Male-content. TC.	*The Malcontent.* 1604. *Pl.* 70.
		* Sir W. D'Avenant. Man is the Master. C.	1669. *Pl.* 29.
Manhood and mis rule.	Manhood and wisdom. C.	Manhood & Wisdome.	Not otherwise known.
		*Sr. Martin-mar-all. C.	[*Sir Martin Mar-all.* John Dryden. 1668.]
		* Mrs. Boothby. Marcelia.	[1670.]
Mariamne Tragedy.	M a r i a m e. T. *Lady Eliz. Carew.*	*Lad. Eliz. Carew.* Marian. T. 1661] Mariam.	*Mariam.* 1613. *Pl.* 15.
		*M. W. Marriage Broker. C.	[In *Gratiæ Theatrales,* 1662.]
		*L. Vis. Faukland. Marriage night. T.	Henry Cary. 1664. *Pl.* 17. See *Corrigenda.*
		Rich. Flecknoe. Marriage of Oceanus and Britannia. M.	[1659.]
		Marriage of Wit & Science. I.	n.d. *Pl.* 140.
Mariage of wit and wisdome.			Apparently printed in 1579, but now only known in MS.
M a r t y r d souldier, *Sherly.*	Martyred souldier. C. *Henry Shirly.*	*Hen. Shirley.* Martyr'd Souldier. T.	1638. *Pl.* 105.

Rogers and Ley, 1656.	*Archer*, 1656.	*Kirkman*, 1661 and 1671.	REMARKS.
Mary Magdelens repentance, *B.H.*	Mary Magdalents. [*sic.*] Repentance. I.	Mary Magdalen's Repentance.	*Life and Repentence of Mary Magdalen.* Lewis Wager 1566. *Pl.* 116.
	Masquard D ciel. M.	*J. S.* Masquarde du Ci'el. M.	*Masquarade du Ciel.* J. (Iohn Sadler?) 1640. N-properly dramatic.
Massacre of Paris.	Massacre of Paris. T. *Christopher Marlow.*	*Chr. Marloe.* Massacre at Paris. T.	n.d. *Pl.* 69.
Massalina, *Rich.*	Massalina. T. *Nath. Richards.*	*Nat. Richards.* Messalina. T.	1640. *Pl.* 89.
Match at midnight.	Match at mid-night. C. *Will. Rouly.*	*Will. Rowley.* Match at Midnight. T. 1661] C.	1633. *Pl.* 90.
Match me in London.	Match me in London. C. *Thomas Barker.*	*Tho. Decker.* Match me in London. C.	1631. *Pl.* 34.
May day, *Chapman.*	May day. C. *Gorge Chapman.*	*Geo. Chapman.* May Day. C.	1611. *Pl.* 20.
		Tho. Midleton. Mayor of Quinborough. C. 1661] The	1661. *Pl.* 80.
Measure for measure, *Shakspear.*	Measure for measure. C. *Will. Shakespear.*	*Will. Shakespear.* Measure for measure. C.	In folio 1623. *Pl.* 94.
Medea.	Medea, Seneca. T.	*John Studley.* Medea. T.	From Seneca. 1566. *Pl.* 9-
		Edw. Sherbourn. Medea. T.	[1648.]
	Menechrims. T.	*W. W.* Menech-.nus. C.	*Menæcmi.* William Warner 1595. *Pl.* 117.

Rogers and Ley, 1656.	Archer, 1656.	Kirkman, 1661 and 1671.	REMARKS.
Marchant of Venice.	Merchant of Venice. C. *William Shakespeare.*	*Will. Shakespear.* Merchant of Venice. C.	1600. *Pl.* 98.
Mercurius Brittanicus, *Brathwat.*		Mercurius Britannicus. C.	*Richard Brathwait. 1641. *Pl.* 13.
		* *Ben. Johnson.* Mercury Vindicated. M.	In folio 1616. *Mq.* 12.
		Bottom the Weaver. I.	[*The Merry-conceited Humours of Bottom the Weaver.* Robert Cox. In *Wits,* 1672.]
	Merry divell of Edmond. C. *William Shakespeare.*	*Will. Shakespear.* Merry Devil of Edmonton. C.	Author unknown. 1608.
	Merry wives of windsor. C. *William Shakespear.*	*Will. Shakespear.* Merry wives of Windsor. C.	1602. *Pl.* 99.
	Metamorphosied Gypsy. M.	*Ben. Johnson.* Metamorphosed Gypsies. M.	In ' Horace his Art of Poetry, &c.,' 1640. *Mq.* 14.
Michaelmas Terme, *Chapman.†*	Michaelmas tearm. C. *Thomas Middleton.*	*Tho. Midleton.* Michaelmas term. C.	*1607. *Pl.* 77.
Microcosmus, *Nabs.*	Microcosmus. M. *Tho. Nabbs.*	*Tho. Nabs.* Microcosmus. M.	*Microcosmus, a Moral Masque.* 1637. *Pl.* 82.
Midsommer nights dream.	Midsommer nights dream. C. *William Shakespear.*	*Will. Shakespear.* Midsomer nights Dream. C.	1600. *Pl.* 99.
Mirza, Barron.	Mercya. T. *Robert Barron.*	*Rob. Baron.* Mirza. T.	[n.d. (c. 1650)].

† Chapman's name found its way in here from the *Gray's Inn Masque,* which comes next on the list.

Rogers and Ley, 1656.	*Archer,* 1656.	*Kirkman,* 1661 *and* 1671.	REMARKS.
Misery of enforct marriage.	Misery of marriage. C. *Georg Wilkins.*	*Geo. Wilkins.* Miseries of enforced Marriage. TC.	1607. *Pl.* 120.
		Nich. Trotte. Arthur. T.	*The Misfortunes of Arthur.* Thomas Hughes. In 'Certain devices and shews,' 1587. *Pl.* 54. Nicholas Trotte contributed the introduction.
		*Tho. Jordain. Money is an Asse. C.	1668. *Pl.* 58.
		Tho. Midleton. More dissemblers than Women. C.	*More dissemblers besides Women.* In 'Two new Plays,' 1657. *Pl.* 77.
	Mortimer's fall. H.	*Ben. Johnson.* Mortimer's fall. T.	A fragment in Vol. II of folio 1640. *Pl.* 55.
Mother Bomby, *Lilly.*	Mother Bomby. C. *John Lilly.*	*John Lilly.* Mother Boniby. C. 1661] Bomby.	*Mother Bomby.* 1594. *Pl.* 65.
		* Tho. Thompson. Mother Shipton's Life & Death. C.	[*The Life of Mother Shipton.* Thomas Thompson. n.d.]
	Mother Rumming. C.		Nothing is known of the play beyond this entry. Could it be a mistake for *Mother Shipton?*
Monsier D'Oliva. *Chap.*	Mounsier de Oliva T.	*George Chapman.* Monsieur D'Olive. C.	1606. *Pl.* 19.
Monsier Thomas, *B.F.*	Mounsieur Thomas. T. *John Fletcher.*	*John Fletcher.* Monsieur Thomas. C.	1639. *Pl.* 10.

Rogers and Ley, 1656.	*Archer,* 1656.	*Kirkman,* 1661 *and* 1671.	REMARKS.
Mucidorus.	Mucidorus. C. *Will. Shakespeare.*	*Will. Shakespeare.* Mucedorus. C.	Author unknown. 1598. *Pl.* 127.
Much adoe about nothing.	Much a doe about nothing. C. *Will. Shakespear.*	*Will. Shakespear.* Much adoe about Nothing. C.	1600. *Pl.* 99.
		* *Sr. Ch. Sidley.* Mulberry garden. C.	[1668.]
Muses looking glasse. *Randolph.*	Muses looking-glass. C. *Tho. Randalph.*	*Tho. Randal.* Muses Looking-glass. C. 1661] *Randoll.*	Thomas Randolph. In 'Poems,' 1638. *Pl.* 86.
Mustapha. *Lord Brooks.*	Mustaphus. T.	*Lord Brooks.* Mustapha. T.	Fulke Greville, Baron Brooke. 1609. *Pl.* 45.
		**Earl of Orrery.* Mustapha. T.	[1668.]
Midas, *Lilly.*	Mydas. T. *John Lilly.*	*John Lilly.* Mydas. C.	1592. *Pl.* 65.
	Neptunes tryumph. M.	*Ben. Johnson.* Neptune's Triumph. M.	n.d. *Mq.* 15.
Claudius tiberius nero.	Nero's life and death. H.	Nero's Life and Death. T.	1607. *Pl.* 134.
Nero Tragedy.	Ne'r new written. C.	Nero newly written. T.	1624. *Pl.* 136.
Play of the Netherlands.			This piece does not appear to be otherwise known.
		Rich. Brome. New Academy, or the New Exchange. C. 1661] The	In 'Five new Plays,' 1659. *Pl.* 14.
New custome.	New custom. C.	New Custom. I.	1573. *Pl.* 123.

Rogers and Ley, 1656.	Archer, 1656.	Kirkman, 1661 and 1671.	REMARKS.
New Inne, *Johnson.*	New Inn. C. *F. B. Jo. F.*	*Ben. Johnson.* New Inne. C.	1631. *Pl.* 58.
{ New trick to cheat the Devil. Trick to cheat the Devil.	New trick to cheat the divel. C.	New trick to cheat the Devil. C.	Robert Davenport. 1639. *Pl.* 30.
	New way to pay old debts. C. *Phil. Massinger.*	*Phil. Massenger.* New way to pay Old Debts. C.	1633. *Pl.* 74.
Woman never vext.	Woman never vext. C. *Wil. Rouly.*	*Will. Rowley.* Wonder a woman never vext. C.	*A New Wonder, a Woman never Vexed.* 1632. *Pl.* 90.
		B e n. J o h n s o n. News from the New World in the Moon. M.	In Vol. II of folio 1640. *Mq.* 13.
Nice valour or the passionate madman.	Nice valour. C. *F. B. John Fletcher.*	*John Fletcher.* Nice Valor, or the Passionate mad-man. C.	In folio 1647. *Pl.* 3.
	Nice wanton. C.	Nice wanton.	1560. *Pl.* 122.
		* *John Dancer.* Nichomede. TC.	[1671. Contains Kirkman's second list.]
Night walker.	Night walker. C. *F.B. Jo. F.*	*John Fletcher.* Night Walker, or the little Thief. C.	1640. *Pl.* 11.
Ninives repentance.	Niniveehs repentance. I.		Not otherwise known.
No body and some body.	No body, and some body. C.	No body & some body. H.	n.d. *Pl.* 140.
		Tho. Midleton. No Wit }like a womans. C. Help {	1657. *Pl.* 80.

Rogers and Ley, 1656.	*Archer,* 1656.	*Kirkman,* 1661 and 1671.	REMARKS.
oble Gentlemen. B.F.	Noble gentleman. C. *F.B. Jo. F.*	*John Fletcher.* Noble Gentleman. C.	In folio 1647. *Pl.* 3.
		*Sr. W. Lower. Noble ingratitude. TC.	1659. *Pl.* 63.
	Noble Souldier. T. *Sam. Rowly.*	*Sam. Rowley.* Noble Spanish Souldier. T.	1634. *Pl.* 90.
oble stranger, *Sherly.*	Noble Stranger. C. *Lewis Machen.*	Noble Stranger. C.	Lewis Sharpe. 1640. *Pl.* 104.
orthern lasse, *Brome.*	Northern lasse. C. *Rich. Brome.*	*Rich. Brome.* Northern Lass. C.	1632. *Pl.* 14.
	Northward ho. C.	*Decker & Webster.* Northward hoe. C.	1607. *Pl.* 34.
ovella, *Brome.*	Novella. C. *Richard Broome.*	*Rich. Brome.* Novella. C.	In 'Five new Plays,' 1653. *Pl.* 13.
	Peleus and Thetis. M.	*James Howel.* Peleus and Thetis. M.	[*The Nuptials of Peleus and Thetis.* 1654.]
	Oberon. M.	**Ben Johnson.* Oberon the Fairy Prince. M.	In folio 1616. *Mq.* 12.
		Sr. Asten Cockain. Obstinate Lady. C.	1657. *Pl.* 22.
ctavias Tragedy.	Octavia. T. *Tho. Newman.*	*T. Nuce.* Octavia. T.	From Seneca. 'by T. N.' n.d. *Pl.* 93. 'Newman' in Archer's list is presumably a mistake for 'Newton,' *i.e.*, the translator of the *Thebais* in the 1581 Seneca.

Rogers and Ley, 1656.	*Archer,* 1656.	*Kirkman,* 1661 and 1671.	REMARKS.
Ædipus.	AEdipus. T.	*Alex. Nevile.* Oedipus. T.	1563. *Pl.* 93.
		Tho. May. Old Couple. C. 1661] The	1658. *Pl.* 76.
Fortunatos.	Fortunatus. C. *Thomas Barker.*	*Tho. Decker.* Fortunatus. C.	*Old Fortunatus.* 1600. *Pl.* 32.
	Old Law. C. *Philip Massinger.*	*Midleton & Rowly.* Old Law. C.	Massinger, Middleton & Rowley. 1656. *Pl.* 74. Contains Archer's list.
Old wifes tales.	Old wives tale. H.	Old Wives Tale.	George Peele. 1595. *Pl.* 85.
	Oldcastles life. H.	*Will. Shakespear.* Old-Castle's Life and Death. H.	*Sir John Oldcastle.* Pseudo-Shak. 1600. *Pl.* 102.
Opportunity, *Sherly.*	Opportunity. C. *Iames Shirly.*	*James Shirley.* Opportunity. C.	1640. *Pl.* 109.
Ordinary, *Cartwright.*	Ordinary. C.	*W. Cartwright.* Ordinary. C.	In col. ed. 1651. *Pl.* 17.
Orestes.	Orestes. T. *Thomas Goffe.*	*Tho. Goffe.* Orestes. T.	1633. *Pl.* 42.
		L. W. Orgula, or the fatal Errour. T.	[1658.]
Orlando furioso.	Orlando furioso. T.	Orlando Furioso. H.	*Robert Greene. 1594. Pl.* 44.
		*Sr. W. Killigrew. Ormazdes. TC.	[1665.]
	{Ortenas. T. {Ortenus. C.		I can only suggest *Hercules Œtæus* already misprinted "Hercules Orteus" in this list.

Rogers and Ley, 1656.	*Archer,* 1656.	*Kirkman,* 1661 *and* 1671.	REMARKS.
		Lod. Carlile. Osmond the great Turk, or the Noble Servant. T.	In 'Two new Plays' 1657. *Pl.* 16.
Moor of Venice, Shakspear.	Othello. T. *Will. Shakespeare.*	*Will. Shakespear.* Othello, the moor of Venice. T. 1661] Othello Moor of Venice.	1622. *Pl.* 102.
		* Sr. Asten Cockain. Ovid. T.	In 'Poems,' 1662. *Pl.* 22.
	Owle. C.		A Play of this name was bought from Robert Daborne by Henslowe in 1613. The reference may, however, be to Jonson's *Masque of Owls.*
		Ben. Johnson. Masque of Owls. M.	In Vol. II of folio 1640. *Mq.* 12.
Conspiracy, *Killegrew.*	Pallanthus and Eudora. T. *Henry Killegrew.* Conspiracie. T. *Henry kellingrew.*	*Hen. Killigrew.* Pallantus & Eudora. T.	(*The Conspiracy.* 1638.) *P. & E.* 1653. *Pl.* 58.
		Ben. Johnson. Pans Anniversary. M.	In Vol. II of folio 1640 *Mq.* 12.
		* Sr. W. Killigrew. Pandora. C.	[1664.]
Fanne, *Marstone.*	Fanne. C. *John Marston.*	*John Marston.* Fawne. C.	*Parasitaster, or the Fawn.* 1606. *Pl.* 71.
		John Heywood. Play between the Pardoner & the Frier, the Curate & Neighbour Prat. I. 1661] A	*** 1533. *Pl.* 47.

Rogers and Ley, 1656.	Archer, 1656.	Kirkman, 1661 and 1671.	REMARKS.
	Paria. P.		[A latin play by Thomas Vincent. 1648.]
	Parlament of Bees. C. *John Day.*	*Jo. Day.* Parliament of Bees. M. 1661] The	1641. *Mq.* 6.
		Tho. Killigrew. Parsons wedding. C.	In folio 1664. *Pl.* 59.
Passionate lovers two parts.	Passionate lovers, both parts. C. *Lodowick Loyd.*	*Lod. Carlile.* Passionate Lovers, 1st. part. TC. *Lod. Carlile.* Passionate Lovers, 2d. part. TC.	1655. *Pl.* 16.
Pastor fido 12.	[Faithfull Shepheardesse. C. *John Dymmocke.*]	Faithful Shepherd. P.	*Il Pastor Fido or the Faithful Shepherd.* 1602. Archer's list has confused this with Fletcher's play; but the attribution is interesting. It was by a relation of Sir Edward Dymock's, whose name, however, is not given. The entry in Rogers' list I take to mean an edition in 12mo., *i.e.,* the 1633 edition of the " Dymock " translation.
Faithfull shepheard.	Faithfull Shepheard. C. *Richard Fanshaw.*	*Rich. Fanshaw.* Faithfull Shepherd. P. 1661] The	[*Il Pastor Fido.* 1647.]
	Pastor fido. P. *Richard Fanshaw.*		Probably a duplicate entry of Fanshawe's translation, but the compiler having already confused the " Dymock " translation with Fletcher's *Faithful Shepherdess,* possibly further confused the two translations.

Rogers and Ley, 1656.	Archer, 1656.	Kirkman, 1661 and 1671.	REMARKS.
Pastor Stapilton.			Apparently some translation of the *Pastor Fido*, ascribed to Sir Robert Stapleton. None such, however, is known.
Loves Loadstone.	Loves loadstone. C.	Loves Loadstone. C.	*Pathomachia, or the Battle oj Affections.* 1630. *Love's Loadstone* is the running title. *Pl.* 136.
Patient Grissel.	Patient Grissel, old. C.	Patient Grissel Old. C.	*Dekker, Chettle & Haughton. 1603. *Pl.* 33. On the authority of Henslowe's diary.
	Patient Grissel, new. C.	Patient Grissel. C.	Possibly the puppet show recorded by Pepys in 1667.
Pedlers prophesie.	Pedlers prophesies. C.	Pedlars Prophesie. C. 1661] The	*Robert Wilson (?) 1595. *Pl.* 121.
		Rob. Fraunce. Countess of Pembrook's Ivy Church. P. 1661] The	Containing a translation of Tasso's *Aminta.* 1591. (See *P.'s Ivy-C.*) *Pl.* 38.
Perkin warbek.	Perkin Warbeck. T. *John Foard.*	*John Ford.* Perkin Warbeck. H.	1634. *Pl.* 38.
Philaster, *B. F.*	Phylaster. T. *John Fletcher.*	*John Fletcher.* Philaster. C.	1620. *Pl.* 8.
Philotus, *Daniel.*	Philotas. T. *Samuel Daniel.*	*Sam. Daniel.* Philotas. T.	In 'Certain small Poems,' 1605. *Pl.* 26.
Philotus in Scotch.	Philotas Scotch.†	Philotus Scotch. C.	*Philotus.* Author unknown. 1609. *Mq.* 26.

† At this point in Archer's list there is great confusion among the letters indicating the nature of the play.

L

Rogers and Ley, 1656.	*Archer,* 1656.	*Kirkman,* 1661 *and* 1671.	REMARKS.
Phœnix.	Phœnix. C.	*Tho. Midleton.* Phœnix. C.	*1607. *Pl.* 77.
Phœnix in her flames.	Phœnix in her flames. T. *Wil. Lower.*	*W. Lower.* Phœnix in her Flames. T.	1639. *Pl.* 63.
	Pharmia in Terence. T. *Rich. Bernard.*	Phormio in Terence. C. 1661] Plutimio.	Richard Bernard. In 'Terence in English,' 1598. *Pl.* 12.
Picture, *Messinger.*	Picture. C. *Phil. Massinger.*	*Phil. Massenger.* Picture. C.	1630. *Pl.* 73.
Pilgrim, *B. F.*	Pilgrim. C. *John Fletcher.*	*John Fletcher.* Pilgrim. C.	In folio 1647. *Pl.* 3.
		* *Tho. Killigrew.* Pilgrim. T.	In folio 1664. *Pl.* 59.
Pitty shee's a whore.	Pittie she is a whore. C. *John Foard.*	*John Ford.* Pity she's a whore. T.	1633. *Pl.* 37.
	Platonick lovers. T. *Wil. Davenant.*	*Sr. W. D'Avenant.* Platonick Lovers. C.	1636. *Pl.* 28.
	Pleasure reconciled. M.	*Ben. Johnson.* Pleasure reconcil'd to Virtue. M.	In Vol. II of folio 1640. *Mq.* 12.
	Hey for Honesty. C. *Tho. Randolph.*	*Tho. Randal.* Hey for honesty, down with knavery. C. 1661] *Randoll.*	Πλουτοφθαλμία Πλουτογαμία, *or Hey, &c.* Thomas Randolph. 1651. *Pl.* 88.
Poetaster, *Johnson.*	Poetaster. C. *Ben Johnson.*	*Ben. Johnson.* Poetaster. C.	1602. *Pl.* 57.
	Politician. C. *Iames Shirly.*	*James Shirley.* Polititian. C.	1655. *Pl.* 110.

Rogers and Ley, 1656.	Archer, 1656.	Kirkman, 1661 and 1671.	REMARKS.
		Alex. Green. Polititian cheated. C.	[1663.]
Martyr, *Lower.*	Martyr. T. *Will. Lower.*	*Sir W. Lower.* Martyr. T.	*Polyeuctes, or the Martyr.* 1655. *Pl.* 63.
		Mrs. Kat. Philips. Pompey. T.	[1663.]
		Waler and others. Pompey. T.	[Edmund Waller, Earl of Dorset, Sir Charles Sedley and Sydney Godolphin. 1664.]
	Poor man's comfort. C. *Robert Davborne.*	*Rob. Dawbourne.* Poor man's comfort. C.	Robert Daborne. 1655. *Pl.* 25.
		Robert Nevile. Poor Scholar. C.	[1662. Lowndes and Fleay mention an edition of 1622; if this exists it is a misprint, since Nevile did not take his B.A. degree till 1660.]
		Rich. Carpenter. Pragmatical Jesuite. C.	[n.d.]
		Presbyterian lash. T.C.	[Anon. (Francis Kirkman?) 1661.]
		Dut. of Newcastle. Presence. C.	[In folio 1668.]
		Tho. Nabs. Entertainment on the Prince's birth day. I.	*Presentation for the Prince's Birthday.* With *Spring's Glory.* 1638. *Mq.* 21.
		Geo. Gascoign. Pleasures at Kenelworth Castle. M.	*The Princely Pleasures,* &c. 1576. *Mq.* 9.

Rogers and Ley, 1656.	Archer, 1656.	Kirkman, 1661 and 1671.	REMARKS.
	Combate of Caps. M. *John Mason.*	Combat of Caps. M.	*Princeps Rhetoricus or P machia, the Combat of C* 1648. Not properly drama
		Sr. W. Killigrew. Princess, or Love at first sight. TC.	Thomas Killigrew. In f 1664. *Pl.* 59.
Prisoners, *Killigrew.*	Prisoners. T. *Thomas Killigrew.*	*Tho. Killigrew.* Prisoners. TC.	With *Claracilla.* 16 *Pl.* 59.
		John Wilson. Projectors. C.	[1665.]
Promus and Cassandria.	Promus and Cassandra both parts. P.	Promus & Cassandra, 1st. part. Promus & Cassandra, 2d. part. 1661] Promus and Cassandra, 2 parts.	George Whetstone. 15 *Pl.* 119.
Prophetesse.	Prophetess. P. *John Fletcher.*	*John Fletcher.* Prophetess. C.	In folio 1647. *Pl.* 3.
	Puritan widow. C. *Will. Shakespeare.*	*Will. Shakespear.* Puritan Widow. C. 1661] The	Pseudo-Shak. (*The Puri or the Widow of Wat Street,* 1607.) *The Puri Widow.* In folio 16 *Pl.* 103 & 94.
Pericles Prin[c]e of Tire.	Pyrocles prince of Tyre. T. *Will. Shakespeare.*	*Will. Shakespear.* Pericles Prince of Tyre. H.	Pseudo-Shak. 1609. *Pl.* 1
	Queen. T. *John Fletcher.*		Impossible to identify. Fl cher's name has crept from another entry.
Queens Arcadia, *Daniel.*	Queens Arcadia. T. *Samuel Daniell.*	*Sam. Daniel.* Queens Arcadia. P.	1605. *Pl.* 27.
		Rich. Brome. Queens Exchange. C	1657. *Pl.* 15.

Rogers and Ley, 1656.	Archer, 1656.	Kirkman, 1661 and 1671.	REMARKS.
		*Ben Johnson. Masque of Queens. M.	1609. *Mq.* 14.
		Rich. Brome. Queen & Concubine. C. 1661] The	In 'Five new Plays' 1659. *Pl.* 14.
Queen of Aragon. *Habington.*	Queen of Arragon. T.	*Will. Habington.* Queen of Arragon. TC.	*1640. *Pl.* 45. The ascription originally rests on Kirkman's authority.
Queen of Corinth.	Queen of corinth. T.	*John Fletcher.* Queen of Corinth. C.	In folio 1647. *Pl.* 3.
'ueen or the exel-·ncy her sex.	Queen of her sex. T.	Queen, or Excellency of her Sex. C. 1661.] the excellency	[1653.]
	Raging Turk. T. *Thomas Goffe.*	*Tho. Goffe.* Raging Turk. T.	1631. *Pl.* 42.
Ram Ally.	Ram-Ally. C. *Philip Massenger.*	*Lord Barrey.* Ram Alley, or merry Tricks. C.	Lodowick Barrey. 1611. *Pl.* 3.
Rape of Lucrasse.	Rape of Lucrecia. C. *Tho. Haiwood.*	*Tho. Heywood.* Rape of Lucrece. T.	1608. *Pl.* 51.
	Rebellion. T. *Thomas Rawlins.*	*Tho. Rawlins.* Rebellion. T.	1640. *Pl.* 88.
	Massanello. T.	Massanello. T.	[Not Durfey's play of the name, which did not appear till 1699, but *The Rebellion of Naples, or the Tragedy of Massinello.* Anon. 1649.]

Rogers and Ley, 1656.	Archer, 1656.	Kirkman, 1661 and 1671.	REMARKS.
Renegado.	Renegado. T. *Philip Massinger*.	*Phil. Massenger.* Renegado. C.	1630. *Pl.* 73.
Returne from Pernascus. C.	Return from Parnassus. C.	Return from Parnassus. C.	1606. *Pl.* 133.
Revenge for honour.		*Geo. Chapman.* Revenge for Honour. T.	1654. *Pl.* 21.
Revenge of Bussy, *Damboise*.	Bussey D Amboys Revenge. T. *George Chapman*.	*Geo. Chapman.* Bussy D'Amboys Revenge. T.	The Revenge of Bussy *D'Ambois*. 1613. *Pl.* 20.
Revengers Tragedy.	Revenger. T. *Tournour*.	*Cyril Tourneur.* Revengers Tragedy. T.	*1607. *Pl.* 115.
		Reward for Virtue. C.	[John Fountain. 1661.]
Rodon and Iris knevit.	Rhodon and Iris. P. *Ralph Knevet*.	*Ralph Knevet*. Rhodon & Iris. P.	1631. *Pl.* 60.
Richard the 2.	Richard 2d. T. *Will. Shakespeare*.	*Will. Shakespear.* Richard the Second. H.	1597. *Pl.* 95.
Richard the 3. *Shakspear*.	Richard Third. T. *Will. Shakespeare*.	*Will. Shakespear.* Richard the 3d. H.	1597. *Pl.* 95.
	King and Queen Intert, M.	King and Queens entertainment at Richmond. M.	1636. *Mq.* 28.
		Rivals. C.	*Sir William D'Avenant. 1668. *Pl.* 29. An alteration of the *Two Noble Kinsmen*. The ascription is on the authority of Cademan, the publisher, as reported by Langbaine.

Rogers and Ley, 1656.	Archer, 1656.	Kirkman, 1661 and 1671.	REMARKS.
Rivall friends, *Hausted.*	Rival friends. C. *Peter Haustead.*	*Pet. Haustead.* Rival Friends. C.	1632. *Pl.* 46.
		John Dreyden. Rival Ladies. TC.	[1664.]
Roaring girle, or Mol cutpurse.	Roaring Girle. C. *Thomas Middleton.*	*Tho. Midleton.* Roaring Girle. C.	1611. *Pl.* 78.
Robin conscience.	Robin Conscience. C.	Robin Conscience.	A poetical dialogue, not dramatic, first printed about 1580. (Halliwell). Hazlitt (H. 439) ascribes it to Martin Parker, and gives no edition before 1635.
Robin hoods Comedy used in may games.		Robin Hoods Pastoral May-games.	'A mery geste of Robyn Hoode . . . with a new playe for to be played in Maye games.' n.d. *Pl.* 140.
		Robin Hood and his crew of Souldiers. C.	[1661.]
	Robin Hood, both parts. C.		Unless these are Munday's two plays entered elsewhere as *The Death* and *The Downfall of Robert, Earl of Huntington,* I cannot identify them.
Robin hoods Pastorall.	Robin Hood. P.		'A pastoral pleasant comedie of Robin Hood and Little John' was entered in the S.R. to E. White, May, 14. 1594.
Roman Actor, *Messinger.*	Roman Actor. *William Shakespere.*	*Phil. Massenger.* Roman Actor. T.	1629. *Pl.* 73.
		* *Will. Joyner.* Roman Empress. T.	[1671.]

Rogers and Ley, 1656.	*Archer,* 1656.	*Kirkman,* 1661 *and* 1671.	REMARKS.
		*John Dover. Roman Generals.	[1667.]
Rome and Juliet.	Romeo and Juliet. T. *William Shakespear.*	*Will. Shakespear.* Romeo & Juliet. T.	1597. *Pl.* 96.
Royall king and loyall subject.	Roíal King. T. *Thomas Haywood.*	*Tho. Heywood.* Royal King and Loyal Subject. C.	1637. *Pl.* 53.
	Roial master. C. *James Shirly.*	*Jamès Shirley.* Royal Master. C.	1638. *Pl.* 108.
		*Tho. Shadwel. Royal Shepherdess. TC.	[1669. An alteration of Fountain's *Rewards of Virtue,* q.v.]
Royall slave, *Carthwright.*	Roial slave. T. *William Cartwright.*	*W. Cartwright.* Royal Slave. TC.	1639. *Pl.* 17.
Rule a wife and have a wife, *Fletcher.*	Rule a wife and have a wife. C. *Iohn Fletcher.*	*John Fletcher.* Rule a Wife and have a Wife. C.	1640. *Pl.* 11.
		John Tateham. Rump, or a Mirror, &c. C.	1660. *Pl.* 114.
		Sr. John Suckling. Sad one. T. 1661] The	A fragment in the *Last remains,* 1659. *Pl.* 113.
Sad Shephard, *Johnson.*	Sad shepherd. C.	*Ben. Johnson.* Sad Shepherd. C.	A fragment in Vol. II of folio 1640. *Pl.* 55.
		*E. M. St. Cecily, or the converted Twins. T.	[1666.]
St. Patrick for Irerand. *Sherly.*	Patrick for Ireland. C. *Iames Shirley.*	*James Shirley.* Patrick for Ireland. H.	*St. P. for I.* 1640. *Pl.* 110.

Rogers and Ley, 1656.	Archer, 1656.	Kirkman, 1661 and 1671.	REMARKS.
		Salmacida spolia. I.	Sir William D'avenant. 1639. *Mq.* 6.
Sapho and Phao. *Lilly.*	Sophao and Phao. T. *John Lilly.*	*John Lilly.* Sapho & Phao. C.	1584. *Pl.* 64.
Untrussing the humerous Poet.	Untrussing the humerous poet. C. *Tho. Decker.*	Untrussing the humourous Poet. C. 1661] *Tho. Decker.*	*Satiromastix, or the untrussing of the Humorous Poet.* Thomas Dekker. 1602. *Pl.* 33.
School of Complement.	School of complements. C. *James Shirly.*	*James Shirley.* School of Complements. C.	1631. *Pl.* 107.
Scornfull Lady.	Scornful ladie. C. *John Fletcher.*	*John Fletcher.* Scornful Lady. C.	1616. *Pl.* 5.
Scots Figaries.	Scots figaries. C. *John Tatham.*	*John Tateham.* Scots Figaries. C.	1652. *Pl.* 114.
Scots politick Presbyter.	Scots politick Presbyter. I.		[Anon. 1647.]
Sea Voyage.	Sea-voiage. C. *F. B. Jo. Fl.*	*John Fletcher.* Sea Voyage. C.	In folio 1647. *Pl.* 3.
Secillides a Piscator.	Secillides. T.	Sicelides. P.	*Phineas Fletcher. 1631. *Pl.* 37.
		**John Dreyden.* Maiden Queen. C.	[*Secret Love, or the Maiden Queen.* 1668.]
See me, and see me not.	{ See me, or see me not. C. } Hanns bere pot. (C.	See me and see me not. C.	(*Hans Beer-Pot, his invisible comedy of*) *See me and see me not.* Daudridgecourt Belchier. 1618. *Pl.* 12.
Sejanus, *Johnson.*	Sejanus fall. C. *Ben. Johnson.*	*Ben. Johnson.* Sejanus. T.	1605. *Pl.* 57.
Selanas Tradigy.	Solynus. T. *Thomus Goffe.*	*Tho. Goffe.* Selimus. T.	*Robert Greene. 1594. 'T. G.' 1638. *Pl.* 44. **On** the authority of *England's Parnassus.*

Rogers and Ley, 1656.	*Archer,* 1656.	*Kirkman,* 1661 and 1671.	REMARKS.
		*Sr. W. Killigrew. Selindra. TC.	[1665.]
Seven Champions.	Champions of Christendom. T. *Thomas Kelligren* [sic].	*John Kirke.* Champions of Christendom. H.	*The Seven Champions of Christendom.* 1638. *Pl.* 59.
		*Geo. Etheridge. She wou'd if she cou'd. C.	[1668.]
Shepherds Holiday.	Shepherds holyday. C. *Joseph Rutter.*	*Jos. Rutter.* Shepherds holyday. P.	1635. *Pl.* 91.
		Wal. Mountague. Shepherds Paradise. C. 1661] The	1659. *Pl.* 81.
{ Shoemakers Holiday. Gentle craft, *Holiday.*	{ Shoomaker holyday. C. Gentle-craft. C.	Gentle craft. C.	**The Shoemakers' Holiday, or the Gentle Craft.* Thomas Dekker. 1600. *Pl.* 32. On the authority of Henslowe's diary.
Shoemaker a Gentleman.	Shoomaker a gentleman. C.	*Will. Rowley.* Shoomaker a Gentleman. C.	1638. *Pl.* 90.
Sicily and Naples, or the Fatall union.	{ Sicily and Naples. T. Fatal union. C.	Fatal Union. T.	*Sicily and Naples, or the Fatal Union.* Samuel Harding. 1640. *Pl.* 45.
Seidge or Loves Convert.	Siege, or loves convert. C. *William Cartwright.*	*W. Cartwright.* Siege, or Lovers Convert. TC.	In col. ed. 1651. *Pl.* 17.
Siege of Rhodes.		*Sr. W. D'Avenant.* Siege of Rhodes, 1st. part. M.	Pt. I. 1656. Pts. I. & II. 1663. *Pl.* 29.

Rogers and Ley, 1656.	*Archer,* 1656.	*Kirkman,* 1661 and 1671.	REMARKS.
		Sr. W. D'Avenant. Siege of Rhodes, 2d. part. M. 1661] The... *Only one entry ; no mention of two parts.*	
		Sr. W. Killigrew. Siege of Urbin. TC.	[*Siege of Urbino.* In folio 1666.]
Silver Age.	Silver-age. C. *Thomas Haywood.*	*Tho. Heywood.* Silver Age. H.	1613. *Pl.* 51.
	Sisters. C.	*James Shirley.* Sisters. C.	In 'Six new Plays,' 1653. *Pl.* 106.
		Sr. Rob. Stapylton. Slighted Maid. C.	[1663.]
		Dutchess of Newcastle. Sociable Compapanions [*sic*], or the Female wits. C.	[In folio 1668.]
Soliman and Persida.	Solyman and Persida. T.	Solimon & Perseda. C.	1599. *Pl.* 129.
Sophister, A Comedy.	Sophister. T.	Sophister. C.	*Richard Zouch. 1639. Pl.* 121. On no particular authority as it seems ; but *see* Apx. I, p. xxix.
	Ioseph. T. *Hugo Grotius.*	*Fra. Goldsmith.* Joseph. T.	[" Hugo Grotius His Sophompaneas, or Joseph. . . By Francis Goldsmith, Esq." n.d.]
	Sophonisba. H. *John Marston.*	*John Marston.* Sophonisba. T.	*The Wonder of Women, or the tragedy of Sophonisba.* 1606. *Pl.* 71.

Rogers and Ley, 1656.	*Archer,* 1656.	*Kirkman,* 1661 *and* 1671.	REMARKS.
Sophy Tragidy, *Sherly.*	Sophy. T. *Thomas Denham.*	*Tho. Denham.* Sophy. T.	1642. *Pl.* 35.
	Spanish Bawd. C.	Spanish Bawd. TC. 1661] The	*James Mabbe. 1631. *Pl.* 65. By 'Don Diego Puede-Ser,' a recognised pseudonym.
Spanish Curat.	Spanish Curate. C. *F. B. Jo. Fl.*	*John Fletcher.* Spanish Curate. C.	In folio 1647. *Pl.* 3.
Spanish Gypsies.		*Midleton & Rowly.* Spanish Gypsies. C. 1661] The	*The Spanish Gipsy.* 1653. *Pl.* 80.
Hieronimo both parts.	Spanish Tragedie. T. *Tho. Kyte.* Hieronimo, both parts. H. *Will. Shakespeare.*	Hieronymo 1st. part. T. Hieronimo. 2 part. T.	* *The first part of Ieronimo.* Thomas Kyd. 1605. **The Spanish Tragedy (or Hieronimo is mad Again).* Thomas Kyd. 1594. *Pl.* 60 & 61. Kyd's authorship of the *First Part* is very doubtful.
Sparages Garden.	Sparagus Garden. C. R[o]bt. Broom.	*Rich.Brome.* Sparagus Garden. C.	1640. *Pl.* 14.
		* *Abr. Bayly.* Spightful Sister. TC.	[1667.]
Springs glory.	Springs glory. M. Tho. Nabbs.	*Tho. Nabs.* Springs glory. M.	1638. *Mq.* 21.
Staple of Newes.	Staple of News. C. *Ben. Johnson.*	*Ben. Johnson.* Staple of News. C.	In Vol. II of folio 1640. (1631.) *Pl.* 55.
		*Step-mother. TC.	[1664.]
Strange discoveries.	Strange discoverie. C.	*I. G.* Strange Discovery. TC.	Iohn Gough. 1640. *Pl.* 43.

Rogers and Ley, 1656.	Archer, 1656.	Kirkman, 1661 and 1671.	REMARKS.
	Stukelyes life and death. H.	Stukeley's Life & Death. H.	Captain Thomas Stukeley. 1605. Pl. 132.
Dutches of Suffolk.	Dutchess of Suffolk. T. Tho. Haiwood.	Tho. Heywood. Dutchess of Suff. H.	*Thomas Drue. 1631. Pl. 36. On the authority of Sir H. Herbert.
		* Tho. Shadwell. Sullen Lovers, or the Impertinents. C.	[1668.]
Summers last Will and Testament.	Summers last will. C.	Tho. Nash. Summer's last will & Testament. C.	1600. Pl. 83.
		Suns Darling. P.	Ford & Dekker. 1656. Pl. 38.
Supposes, Gascoine.	Supposes. I. George Gascoynd.	Geo. Gascoign. Supposes. C.	In col. ed. 1575. Pl. 40.
		*Sr. Rob. Howard. Surprisal. C.	[1665.]
Susanna.	Susanna's tears. I.	Susanna's Tears.	Not otherwise known. Rogers' entry, however, may refer to the Virtuous & Godly Susanna. Thomas Garter. [1578.] Pl. 39.
Swaggering Damsell, Chamberlen.	Swaggering Damsel. C. Robert Chamberlyne.	Rob. Chamberlain. Swaggering Damsel. C.	1640. Pl. 18.
Swetman, the woman hater arraign'd.	Swetman the womanhater arraigned. C.	Swetnam the womanhater Arraigned. C.	1620. Pl. 136.
	Tale of a tub. C. Ben Johnson.	Ben. Johnson. Tale of a Tub. C.	In Vol. II of folio 1640. Pl. 55.

Rogers and Ley, 1656.	_Archer,_ 1656.	_Kirkman,_ 1661 _and_ 1671	REMARKS.
Tamberlaine, both parts.	Tamerlain, both parts. H.	_Chr. Marloe._ Tamberlain, 1st. part. T. _Chr. Marloe._ Tamberlain, 2d. part. T. 1661.] _Author's name omitted in both cases._	*1592. _Pl._ 67.
Taming of a Shrew. _Shakes :_	Taming of a shrew. C. _Will. Shakespeare._	_Will. Shakespear._ Taming of the Shrew. C.	In folio 1623. _Pl._ 94. The entries are probably all intended for Shakespeare's play.
Tancred and Gismond.	Tancred and Gismond. T.	_Rob. Wilmot._ Tancred & Gismond. T.	1591. _Pl._ 120.
		*_M. Medburn._ Tartuff, or the French Puritan. C.	[1670.]
		*_Tho. St. Serfe._ Tarugoes Wiles, or the Coffe-House. C.	[1668.]
	Marriage of Arts. C.	_Barten Holliday._ Marriage of the Arts. C.	Τεχνογαμία, _or the M. of the A._ 1618. _Pl._ 54.
Tempest, _Shakespeare._	Tempest. C. _Will. Shakespeare._	_Will. Shakespear._ Tempest. C.	In folio 1623. _Pl._ 94
	Temple of love. M.	_Sir W. D'Avenant._ Temple of Love. M. 1661] The	1634. _Mq._ 5.
	Theboies, Seneca. C.	_Tho. Newton._ Thebais. T.	In the 1581 Seneca. _Pl._ 92.

Rogers and Ley, 1656.	*Archer,* 1656.	*Kirkman,* 1661 *and* 1671.	REMARKS.
		Ben. Johnson. Entertainments of King James & Queen Ann, at Theobalds. E.	In folio 1616. *Mq.* 12.
		Ben. Johnson. Entertainments of the King of England and King of Denmark at Theobalds. E.	In folio 1616. *Mq.* 11.
Thiertes Tragedy.	Thertes. T. *Iasper Haiwood.*	*Jasper Heywood.* Thyestes. T.	1560. *Pl.* 93.
Thery and Theodoret.	Thiery and Theodoret. T. *E. B. Jo. Fl.*	*John Fletcher.* Thierry and Theodoret. T.	1621. *Pl.* 8.
Thirtes interlude.	Thirstes, an Interlude.	Thersytes. I.	n.d. *Pl.* 141.
		Tho. Killigrew. Thomaso, or the Wanderer. C.	In folio 1664 (2 parts). *Pl.* 59.
		T. W. Thornby Abbey. T.	[*Thorney Abbey.* In *Gratiæ Theatrales,* 1662.]
		Webster & Rowly. Thracian wonder. H.	In 'Two new Plays,' 1661. *Pl.* 117.
	Ladies of London. C.	*R. W.* Three Ladies of London. C.	Robert Wilson. 1584 *Pl.* 120.
Lawes of nature Moses and Christ.	Lawes of nature. C.	Laws of Nature. C.	*The three Laws of Nature Moses, and Christ.* Iohn Bale. 1538. *Pl.* 2.
Lords and Ladies of London.	Lords of London. C.	*W. R.* Three Lords and Ladies of London. C. 1661] R. W.	Robert Wilson. 159c *Pl.* 121.

Rogers and Ley, 1656.	*Archer,* 1656.	*Kirkman,* 1661 *and* 1671.	REMARKS.
Tide tarries for no man.	Tide tarrieth for no man. C.	*Geo. Wapul.* Tyde tarrieth for no man. C. 1661] The	*The Tide tarrieth no Man.* 1576. *Pl.* 117.
		Ben. Johnson. Time Vindicated to himself & to his Honours. M.	In Vol. II of folio 1640. *Mq.*
Timon of Athens.	Timon of Athens. I.	*Will. Shakespear.* Tymon of Athens. T.	In folio 1623. *Pl.* 94.
Titus and Androni-cus.	Titus Andronicus. T. *Will. Shakes-peare.*	*Will. Shakespear.* Titus Andronicus. T.	1600. *Pl.* 99.
	Tom tyler. C.	Tom Tyler and his Wife. I.	1661. *Pl.* 138. Contains Kirkman's first list.
Totnam Court.	Totenham Court. C. *Thomas Nabbs.*	*Tho. Nabs.* Toten-ham Court. C.	1636. *Pl.* 82.
		Sr. Asten Cockain. Tr[a]polin sup-pos'd a Prince. TC.	In 'Small Poems,' 1658. *Pl.* 22.
Three English Heroes.	Three English heroes. C.	*Day. W. Rowley & Wilkins.* Travails of the three Eng-lish Brothers. H. 1661] The	1607. *Pl.* 31.
	Traitor. T. *Iames Shirly.*	*James Shirley.* Traytor. T.	1635. *Pl.* 108.
	{Trial of Chevalry. C. {Cavalier Dick boies. C.	Tryal of Chivalry. C. 1661] The	1605. *Cavaliero Dick Bowyer.* 1605. *Pl.* 132.
Triall of Treasure.	Trial of treasure. C.	Tryal of treasure.	1567. *Pl.* 123.

Rogers and Ley, 1656.	Archer, 1656.	Kirkman, 1661 and 1671.	REMARKS.
Trick to catch the old one.	Trick to catch the old one. C. *Will. Shakespeare.*	*Tho. Mideton.* Trick to catch the old one. C.	1608. *Pl.* 78.
Triumph of Beauty.	Triumph of beauty. M.	*James Shirley.* Triumph of beauty. M.	In 'Poems,' 1646. *Mq.* 23.
Triumph of peace.	Triumph of peace. M. *Iames Shirly.*	*James Shirley.* Triumph of Peace. M.	1633. *Mq* 23.
		S. Pardidge. Troades. T. 1661.] Pordidge.	[1660.]
Troas.	Troas. T.	*Jasper Heywood.* Troas. T.	1559. *Pl.* 92.
Troiles and Cresida.	Troilus and Cressida. T.	*Will. Shakespear.* Troylus and Cresida. T.	1609. *Pl.* 101.
Fuimus tries the true Trojans.	True Trojans. T.	True Trojans. H.	("Fuimus Troes Ænid, 2.") *The True Troians.* Jasper Fisher, 1633. *Pl.* 37.
		Earl of Orrery. Tryphon. T.	[1669.]
Muliasses the turk.	Muliasses the Turke. T. *John Mason.*	*John Mason.* Muleasses the Turk. T.	*The Turk.* 1610. *Muleasses the Turk.* 1632. *Pl.* 72.
Twelfth night.	Twelfth-night. C. *William Shakespere.*	*Will. Shakespear.* Twelf night, or what you will. C.	In folio 1623. *Pl.* 94.
	Twinns. C. *Wil. Rider.*	*W. Rider.* Twins. TC.	1655. *Pl.* 89.
Angry women of **Abington.**	Angry woman of Abingdon. T. *Henry Porter.*	*Henry Porter.* Angry women of Abington. C.	*The Two Angry Women of Abington.* 1599. *Pl.* 85.

M

Rogers and Ley, 1656.	Archer, 1656.	Kirkman, 1661 and 1671.	REMARKS.
Two Gentlemen of Verona. Gentleman of verona.	Gentleman of Verona. C. *William Shakespeare.*	*Will. Shakespear.* Gentleman of Verona. C. 1661] Gentlemen	*The Two Gentlemen of Verona.* In folio 1623. *Pl.* 94.
Two Noble Kinsmen.	Two noble kinsmen. C. *Will. Shakespear.* Noble Kinsman. C.	*John Fletcher.* Two Noble Kinsmen. TC.	'J. Fletcher & W. Shakespeare.' 1634. *Pl.* 9.
Maids of Mortlake.	Maids of Moreclack. C. *Robert Armion.*	*Rob. Armin.* Maids of Moorclack. H. 1661] The	*The Two Maids of Moreclake.* 1609. *Pl.* 2.
	Merry milk-maids. C.	*J. C.* Merry Milkmaids. C. 1661.] The	*The Two M. M.* 1620. *Pl.* 136.
Two Tragidies in one.	Two Tragedies in one. T. *Roger Yernton*	*Rob. Yarington.* Two Tragedies in one. T.	*Two Lamentable Tragedies.* 1601. *Pl.* 121.
Two wise men, and all the rest fooles.	Two wisemen. C.	*Geo. Chapman.* Two wise men, & all the rest fools. C.	Author unknown. 1619. *Pl.* 136.
		John Dryden. Tyrannick Love, or the Royal Martyr. T.	[1670.]
The Life of *John* the Baptist. (?)		Tyrannical Government.	*Tyrannical Government Anatomized.* Anon. from George Buchanan's Latin play *Baptistes.* 1642.
Unfortunate Lovers. *B. F.*	Unfortunate lovers. C. *Will. Davenant.*	*Sir W. D'Avenant.* Unfortunate Lovers. T.	1643. *Pl.* 28.
Unfortunate Mother.	Unfortunate mother. C. *Thomas Nabs.*	*Tho. Nabs.* Unfortunate Mother. T.	1640. *Pl.* 83.

Rogers and Ley, 1656.	*Archer, 1656.*	*Kirkman, 1661 and 1671.*	REMARKS.
		*Unfortunate Usur- per. T.	[1663.]
		*Ungrateful Fa- vourite. T.	[1664.]
		Gibb. Swinhoe. Fair Irene. T. 1661.] *Gilb. Swin- hoe.* The	[*The Unhappy Fair Irene.* 1658.]
Unnaturall Combat.	Unnatural com- bate. C. *Philip Massenger.*	*Phil. Massenger.* Unnatural combat. T.	1639. *Pl.* 74.
		* *Edw. Howard.* Usurper. T.	[1668.]
Valentine, *Fletcher.*	Valentinian. C. *Iohn Fletcher.*	*John Fletcher.* Val- entinian. T.	In folio 1647. *Pl.* 3.
Valiant Scot.	Valiant Scot. C.	Valiant Scot. T.	'By J. W. Gent.' 1637. *Pl.* 137.
Valiant Welchman.	Valiant Welshman. C.	*R. A.* Valiant Welchman. T.	1615. *Pl.* 135.
	Varieties. C.	*W. Duke of Newca.* Varieties. C. 1661] *Newcastle.*	*The Variety.* William Caven- dish, D. of N. With *Country Captain,* 1649. *Pl.* 18.
	Very woman. C. *Will. E. of New- cast.*†	*Phil. Massenger.* Very Woman. C.	In 'Three new Plays,' 1655. *Pl.* 72.
		Sir Rob. Howard. Vestal Virgin. T.	[1665.]
		T. Porter. Vil- lain. T.	[1663.]

† In Archer's list the author's name has crept in from the entry of the *Varieties.*

Rogers and Ley, 1656.	*Archer,* 1656.	*Kirkman,* 1661 *and* 1671.	REMARKS.
	Virgils Eclogs. T.		What translation is intended I cannot say.
Virgin Martyr.	Virgin martyr. C. *Phillip Massenger.*	*Phil. Massenger.* Virgin Martyr. T.	1622. *Pl.* 72.
Virgin Widdow.	Virgin widow. C. *Francis Quarls.*	*Fra. Quarles.* Virgin Widdow. C.	1649. *Pl.* 86.
{ Vertuous Octavia. { Octavias Tragi-Co-{ medy.	Virtuous Octavia. T. *Phillip Mas-senger.*† Octavias. T. *Tha-mas Brandon.*	*Sam Brandon.* Virtuous Octavia. TC. 1661] The	1598. *Pl.* 13.
	Vision of delight. M.	*Ben. Johnson.* Vi-sion of delight. M.	In Vol. II of folio 1640. *Mq.* 12.
		Sam. Daniel. Vi-sion of the 12. god-desses. M.	1604. *Mq.* 4.
Vow-breaker, *Samp-son.*	Vow breaker. C. *Will. Sampson.*	*Will. Sampson.* Vow-breaker. T.	1636. *Pl.* 91.
Fox, *B. Johnson.*	Fox. C. *Ben. John-son.*	*Ben. Johnson.* Fox. C.	*Vulpone.* 1607. *The Fox.* In folio 1616. *Pl.* 57.
		Tho. Jordain. Walks of Islington & Hogsdon. C. 1661] The	1657. *Pl.* 58.
Albertus walenstine. *Glapthorn.*	Albertus Walenstein. T.	*Hen. Glapthorne.* Albertus Wallen-stein. T.	1639. *Pl.* 41.
		Tho. Meriton. Wandring lover. TC. 1661] The	[1658].

† In Archer's list the author's name has crept in from the entry of the *Very Woman.*

Rogers and Ley, 1656.	Archer, 1656.	Kirkman, 1661 and 1671.	REMARKS.
Warning for fair women.	Warning for fair women. C.	Warning for fair Women. T.	1599. *Pl.* 129.
Cæser and Pompey. *Chapman.*	Cæsar and Pompey. T. *George Chapman.*	*Geo. Chapman.* Cæsar & Pompey. T.	1631. *Pl.* 21.
Cyrus King of Persia.	Cyrus K. of Persia.	Cyrus King of Persia. T.	*The Wars of Cyrus.* 1594. *Pl.* 126.
Weakest goes to the wall.	Weakest goeth to the Wall. C.	Weakest goes to the wall. C.	1600. *Pl.* 130.
Wealth and health.	Wealth and health. C.	Wealth & health.	n.d. *Pl.* 141.
	Play of the weather. C.	*John Heywood.* Play of the weather. I. 1661] The	1533. *Pl.* 47.
Wedding, *Shirley.*	Wedding. C. *Nath. Field.*†	*James Shirley.* Wedding. C.	1629. *Pl.* 106.
		Ben. Johnson. Kings Entertainment at Welbeck. M.	In Vol. II of folio 1640. *Mq.* 13.
Westward hoe.	Westward ho. C. *John Webster.*	*Decker & Webster.* Westward hoe. C.	1607. *Pl.* 34.
What you will, *Marston.*	What you will. C. *John Marston.*	*John Marston.* What you will. C.	1607. *Pl.* 71.
	When you see me, you will know me. C. *Sam. Rowly.*	*Sam. Rowley.* When you see me you know me. H.	1605. *Pl.* 89.
	White divel. C. *John Webster.*	*John Webster.* White Devil. T.	1612. *Pl.* 117.

† In Archer's list the author's name in this entry has got interchanged with that of *Woman is a Weathercock.*

Rogers and Ley, 1656.	Archer, 1656.	Kirkman, 1661 and 1671.	REMARKS.
Whore of *Babylon.*	Whore of Babylon. C. *Tho. Dekker.*	*Tho. Decker.* Whore of Babylon. C.	1607. *Pl.* 34.
Wiats History.	Wiats historie. H. *Tho. Decker.*	*Decker & Webster.* Wiat's History. H.	*Sir Thomas Wyat.* 1607. *Pl.* 34.
Widdow, by *Midleton.*	Widow. C. *Thomas Middleton.*	*Midleton & Rowly.* Widdow. C.	Ionson, Fletcher & Middleton. 1652. (*see* Middleton.) *Pl.* 79.
Widdowes tear.	Widows tears. C. *George Chapman.*	*Geo. Chapman.* Widdow's tears. C.	1612. *Pl.* 20.
Wife for a month.	Wife for a month. C. *F. B. Jo. Fletcher.*	*John Fletcher.* Wife for a month. C.	In folio 1647. *Pl.* 3.
		*John Dryden. Wild Gallant. C.	[1669.]
Wild Goose Chase.	Wild-goose chase. C. *F. B. Jo. Flet.*	*John Fletcher.* Wild-goose chase. C.	1652. *Pl.* 11.
Wily beguild.	Wylie beguiled. C.	Wily beguiled. C.	1606. *Pl.* 133.
Wine, Beer, and Ale.	Wine, Beer, Ale, Tobacco. C. Ale, Beer, Tobacco, C.	Wine, Beer, Ale, and tobacco. I.	*W. B. and A.* 1629. *W. B. A. & T.* 1630. *Mq.* 27. The first edition purports to be by Mercurius Brittanicus, a pseudonym used by Braithwait.
Winters Tale.	Winters tale. C. *Wil. Shakespear.*	*Will. Shakespear.* Winters tale. C.	In folio 1623. *Pl.* 94.
Dr. Dottipo.	Doctor bodipoll. C.	Doctor Dodipol. C.	*The Wisdom of Doctor D.* 1600. *Pl.* 130.
Wise woman of Hogsdon. *Heywood*	Wise woman of Hogsdon. C. *Thomas Haywood.*	*Tho. Heywood.* Wise woman of Hogsdon. C.	1638. *Pl.* 53.
Wit at severall weapons.	Wit at several weapons. C. *F. B. Jo. Fletcher.*	*John Fletcher.* Wit at several Weapons. C.	In folio 1647. *Pl.* 3.

Rogers and Ley, 1656.	*Archer,* 1656.	*Kirkman,* 1661 *and* 1671.	REMARKS.
Wit in a Constable.	Wit in a Constable. C. *Hen. Glapthorn.*	*Hen. Glapthorne.* Wit in a Constable. C.	1640. *Pl.* 41.
Wit of a woman.	Wit in a woman. C.	Wit of a woman. C.	1604. *Pl.* 132.
Wit without mony. *B. F.*	Wit without money. C. *F. B. Jo. Fl.*	*John Fletcher.* Wit without money. C.	1639. *Pl.* 10.
Wits. *W: Daven:*	Witts. C. *Wil. Dovenant.*	*Sr. W. D'Avenant.* Wits. C	1636. *Pl.* 28.
		Rowley, Decker, & *Ford.* Witch of Edmonton. TC. 1661] The	1658. *Pl.* 90.
		**T. P.* Witty Combat. TC.	[Thomas Porter. 1663.]
	Wittie fair one. C. *Iames Shirley.*	*James Shirley.* Witty fair one. C.	1633. *Pl.* 107.
Womans hater.	Woman-hater. C. *F. B. Jo. Fl.*	*John Fletcher.* Woman-hater. C.	1607. *Pl.* 4.
Woman in the moon.	Woman in the moon. C. *John Lilly.*	*John Lilly.* Woman in the Moon. C. 1661] The	1597. *Pl.* 65.
Woman kill'd with kindnesse.	Woman kill'd with kindness. C. *Thomas Haywood.*	*Tho. Heywood.* Woman kill'd with kindness. C.	1607. *Pl.* 50.
Woman is a weathercock.	Woman is a weathercock. C. *Iames Shirley.*†	*Nat. Field.* Woman's a weathercock. C.	1612. *Pl.* 36.
		**Edw. Howard.* Woman's Conquest. TC.	[1671.]

† In Archer's list the author's name in this entry has got interchanged with that of the *Wedding.*

Rogers and Ley, 1656.	*Archer,* 1656.	*Kirkman,* 1661 and 1671.	REMARKS.
Woman's prize.	Womans prize. C. *F. B. Jo. Fletcher.*	*John Fletcher.* Womans Prize, or the tamer tam'd. C.	In folio 1647. *Pl.* 3.
		Tho. Midleton. Women beware Women. T.	In 'Two new Plays,' 1657. *Pl.* 77.
Woman pleasd, or the Tamer tam'd.	Woman pleasd. C. *F. B. Jo. Fletcher.*	*John Fletcher.* Women pleased. C.	In folio 1647. *Pl.* 3.
Wonder of a Kingdome.	Wonder of a Kingdom. C. *Tho. Decker.*	*Tho. Decker.* Wonder of a Kingdom. C.	1636. *Pl.* 35.
World lost at Tennis.	World tost at tennis. C. *Thomas Midelton.*	*Tho. Midleton.* World tost at Tennis. M. 1661] World lost	Middleton & Rowley. 1620. *Mq.* 17.
		H. H. B. Plutus. C.	[*The World's Idol, Plutus.* 1659.]
Marius and Scilla.	Marius and Scilla. T. *Tho. Lodge.*	*Tho. Lodge.* Marius & Scylla. T.	*The Wounds of Civil War or Marius and Scilla.* 1594. *Pl.* 62.
Yorkshire Tragidy.	Yorkshire Tragedie. T. *Will. Shakespeare.*	*Will. Shakespear.* Yorkshire Tragedy. T.	Pseudo-Shake. 1608. *Pl.* 103.
Young Admirall.	Young Admiral. C. *James Shirley.*	*James Shirley.* Young Admiral. C.	1637. *Pl.* 108.
Your faire Gallants.	Your fine gallants. C. *Thomas Midelton.*	*Tho. Midleton.* Your five Gallants. C.	n.d. *Pl.* 81.
	Enterlude of youth. I.	Interlude of Youth. I.	n.d. *Pl.* 141.
FINIS	FINIS.		

A LIST OF ENGLISH PLAYS.

ADDENDA & CORRIGENDA.

Introduction. page ix. line 4. *For* all the works, *read* all the dramatic works.

P. 2. Bale. *Three Laws.* n.d. In place of the present entry, read :
A Comedy concernynge thre lawes, of nature, Moses, & Christ, corrupted by the Sodomytes Pharysees and Papystes. Compiled by Johan Bale. Anno M.D.XXXVIII. [*Colophon :*] *lately imprented per Nicolaum Bamburgensem.* 8vo. 𝕭.𝕷.
> With a woodcut portrait of the author at the end of the play on sig. G1.
> (B.M. (C. 34. a. 12., wanting titlepage). Bodl.

P. 4. Beaumont and Fletcher. *The Woman Hater.* 1607. *For* *[Another edition.] *read* *[Another issue.] *and add note :* The sheets of the above issued with the titlepage altered.

The Woman Hater. 1649. *Add note :* The sheets of 1648 re-issued with a new titlepage and preliminary matter.

P. 6. *The Maid's Tragedy.* 1650. Note that a publisher's advertisement on the verso of the last leaf was printed in 1660, and that consequently the date on the titlepage *may* be a misprint. (*See* Apx. I, p. xxxii).

P. 8. *Philaster.* 1652. In place of this entry, read :
Philaster : [&c.] The fifth Impression. *for William Leake.* 1652.
> B.M. (644. d. 21.)

Philaster [&c.] The fifth Impression. *for William Leake.* 1652.
> Dyce. Bodl.

P. 9. *Thierry and Theodoret.* 1649. *Add note :* The sheets of 1648 re-issued with a new titlepage and preliminary matter.

P. 14. R. Brome. *Five New Plays.* 1659. There is only one edition of this collection, not two as I supposed. There are, however, alternative title-pages to the *English Moor*, one without author's name, dated 1658, the other with the author's name, dated 1659. Both the copies in the B. M. are imperfect, each wanting the preliminary leaves contained in the other. The Thomason copy has the 1658, the Grenville the 1659 titlepage to the *English Moor*. The collation of the preliminary matter should be A^8 a^4. There is a perfect copy in original sheep in the Dyce collection, containing both titlepages to the *English Moor*. Of these the one dated 1659 is, I believe, a cancel printed on a4, while that dated 1658 occupies A1 (of the play).

P. 16. Carlell. *The Passionate Lovers.* 1655. The quarto and octavo issues of this date are printed from the same setting up of the type, the arrangement of the pages in the frame alone being altered. There are copies of both issues in the Bodleian.

P. 17. Cary. *The Marriage Night.* This play has no claim whatever to be included. It was written by Henry Cary, Viscount Falkland, correctly identified by Langbaine as the father of the then Viscount (Anthony). This Henry, who died in 1663, was fourth Viscount Falkland, having succeeded his brother Lucius in 1649. Most writers who mention the play have confused the author with his father, the second Viscount, who fell at Newbury in 1643. His name, however, was Lucius, and not Henry, though it is true that he is sometimes called by both names together, perhaps by confusion. Henry, first Viscount, died in 1633. The play is rightly assigned in the *Biographia* of 1812, though the author has been confused with his brother under the corporate name of Henry Lucius, who is said to have been the *only* son of "the great Lord Falkland." Mr. Hazlitt (*Dodsley,* xv) also calls the author the son of "the great Lord Falkland," but proceeds to give 1643 as the date of his death. In this he is followed by Mr. Fleay (*Chronicle History,* II, 368). It is correctly, though not very clearly assigned by Dr. Ward (*Eng. Dr. Lit.* IV, 335).

P. 19. Chapman. *Eastward Ho.* 1605. Note. *For* "oppos'd" *read* "opposd."

[Another edition.] 1605. Note. *For* "oppos'de" *read* "opposde." The Dyce copy of this edition contains the duplicate leaves E and E2, which were cancelled owing to the passages which gave offence to James and led to the imprisonment of the authors. This was, therefore, the earlier edition.

Bussy d'Ambois.   1616.   Probably a mistake for 1646, omitted in the *Biographia.*

P. 22.   *Revenge for Honour.*   1654.   Another issue, the imprint alone altered.

Revenge for Honour.   1659.   Another issue, with a new titlepage.

Cokayne.   *Small Poems.*   1658.   This is evidently nothing but an imperfect copy of the next entry, each part of which has a separate titlepage.   There is no reason to suppose that the *Poems* were issued alone.

Poems, 1662.   Omit Dyce from list of copies, and add :
    [Another issue.]   *for Francis Kirkman.*   1662.
        Dyce.

P. 26.   Daniel.   *Certain Small Works.*   1607.   After this entry add :
    [Another issue.]   *I. W. for Simon Waterson.*   1607.
        The sheets of the above re-issued with cancels for the separate titlepages to
        Cleopatra and *Musophilus,* adding dedications.
            Huth.

The Whole Works.   1623.   Note.   *Add :* It was edited by John Daniel, brother of the poet.

P. 27.   *The Queen's Arcadia.*   1605.   Prefix asterisk (*).

D'avenant.   *Two Plays.*   Note.   *For* "Gabriel" *read* "Gabriel Bedel." The signatures are continuous.

Works.   Contains an engraved portrait by Farthorne (wanting in B.M. copy).

P. 29.   *The Siege of Rhodes.*   *Add :* [Another edition.]   *for Henry Herring- man.*   1670.
        Hazlitt. II. 159.

P. 32.   Richard Day.   *Christ Jesus Triumphant.*   I have been unable to find any copy of this translation, but a modern reprint in the B.M. is not dramatic.   There is certainly a Latin play of the title by Fox (Basel, 1556), but I doubt whether the present "treatise" is a translation of it.

P. 39.   Garter.   *Susanna.*   This entry should be omitted.   The authority for the existence of the work, beyond the entry in the S.R., is a MS. note by Thomas Coxeter in a copy of Jacob's Lives.   Nothing has been heard of it for more than a century and a half.

P. 41. Gascoigne. *Glass of Government.* This is the same edition as the previous entry, differing only on the last page. It is, however, the earlier issue, and wants the list of *errata* following the colophon in the later.

Glapthorne. *Wallenstein.* 1640. This is not another edition, but a re-issue with the imprint alone altered.

P. 43. Gough. *The Strange Discovery.* 1640. Second entry. This is a re-issue of the sheets of the first, with the name alone altered.

P. 45. Greville. *Mustapha.* 1609. Prefix asterisk (*).

Haughton. *Englishmen for my Money.* 1626. Prefix asterisk (*).

P. 47. John Heywood. *The Pardoner and the Friar.* 1533. *For* frere, *read* frere/

P. 48. Thomas Heywood. *Edward IV.* 1600. *Add :* 𝕭.𝕷.

P. 50. *If you know not me.* Part II. 1632. *For* we *read* me. In the three copies of this edition in the B.M. the imprint has been clipt by the binder, and it is impossible to say whether the date is 1632 or 1633. The catalogue gives 1633. In two cases it is bound with the 1632 edition of Part I, in one case with the 1639 edition.

P. 52. *The Fair Maid of the West.* 1631. Each part has separate signatures, and the second is without pagination.

The Iron Age. Part I. 1632. *Add:* [Another issue.] Written by Thomas Heywood. *Nicholas Okes.* 1632.

> The sheets of the above issued with a printer's device replacing the woodcut on the titlepage. That the titlepages are alternative and not, as Hazlitt says, duplicate (*Old English Plays*, 4) is shown by the fact that each has the list of *personæ* on the verso printed from the same setting up of the type.
>
> W. W. G.

P. 55. Jonson. *Workes.* 1616. Second issue. Note, l. 1. *For* impress, *read* imprint.

P. 56. *Works.* 1692. Contains engraved portrait by Elder.

P. 57. *The Case is altered.* 1609. *Add :* [Another issue]. [Anon.] 1609. *See* Gifford and Cunningham's edition, vi. 509.

P. 58. Jordan. *The Walks of Islington and Hogsdon.* 1657. *For* E. 717 (5) *read* E. 910 (5).

Tricks of Youth. This is not another edition, but merely another issue, the titlepage and one leaf being different. The date 1663 has been printed or stamped on to the titlepage after it had been printed off.

P. 60. Knevet. *Rhodon and Iris.* 1631. *Add note:* The author's name appears at the end of the epistle dedicatory.

P. 61. Kyd. *Spanish Tragedy.* "sold by Thomas Langley." 1623. For the reference to Hazlitt, substitute " Huth," and in the next entry: *for* *[Another edition.] *read* *[Another issue.]

The First Part of Jeronimo. 1605. Prefix asterisk (*). The ascription to Kyd is very doubtful.

P. 66. Markham. *For* GERVAS, *read* GERVASE.

The Dumb Knight. 1633. *Add note:* The preface is again signed, Lewes Machin.

Marlowe. *Tamburlaine.* Insert before first entry :

Tamburlaine the Great. Who, from a Scythian Shepheard by his rare and wonderfule Conquests became a most puissant and mightye Monarque. And (for his tyranny, and terrour in Warre) was tearmed, The Scourge of God. Deuided into two Tragicall Discourses, as they were sundrie times shewed vpon Stages in the Citie of London, By the right honorable the Lord Admyrall, his seruantes. Now first, and newlie published. *Richard Iones.* 1590. 8vo.

> Sigs. A–K in eights, L in twos. The only known copy wants one leaf near the end. A fragment, consisting of the titlepage and address to the reader only is in the Bridgwater Library. It has been described as a quarto, but as it agrees letter for letter with the Bodleian octavo, this is presumably a mistake.
>
> Bodl.

Tamburlaine. 1592. *Add:* 8vo. Note. *Add:* This is a different edition to the octavo of 1590, having sigs. A–I in eights.

Hazlitt (H. 373) boldly asserted that they were identical (compare titles here given !) but that in the B.M. copy "someone has altered the date with a pen to 1592." This is certainly not so, the date can never have been 1590, but I am not sure it has not been altered from 1593 to 1592. Langbain mentions an edition of 1593. Collier seems to have known an edition of 1597 (See Cunningham's Marlow, p. 368).

P. 73.   Massinger.   *The Bondman.*   1638.   ("for Harrison ").   *For* B.L.O., *read* Bodl.

P. 75.   *The City Madam.*   1659.   Another issue, with date alone altered.

May.   *Two Tragedies.*   1654.   This is a re-issue of the separate editions with a general titlepage substituted for that of *Agrippina,* and a new one dated 1654 for that of *Cleopatra.*

P. 76.   Mayne.   The entries should probably be as follows :

Two Plaies.   The City Match.   A Comœdy.   And the Amorous Warre A Tragi-comœdy.   Both long since written, By J. M. of Ch. Ch. in Oxon. *Oxford.   Re-Printed by Hen. Hall, Rich. Davis.* [sic]   1658.   4to.

> This volume contains the 1648 *Amorous War,* sometimes (*e.g.* B.M.) with the original titlepage, sometimes (*see* Hazlitt, II, 390) with a new titlepage dated 1659.
>
> B.M. (1346. c. 2.)   Bodl. (impf.)

[Another edition.]   *Oxford.*   [&c.]   1659.   8vo.

> This volume contains the two separate editions of this date, which have, however, distinct signatures, &c., preceded by a general titlepage.
>
> Haz. H. 385.

----

* The Citye Match.   A Comœdye.   Presented to the King and Queene at White-Hall.   Acted   since   at   Black-Friers, by   His   Maiesties   Servants. *Oxford.   Leonard Lichfield.*   M.DC.XXXIX.   Fol.

> B.M. (644. k. 29.)   Bodl.

[Another edition.]   By J. M. St : of Ch : Ch : in Oxon.   *Oxford, Henry Hall, for Rich : Davis.*   1659.   8vo.

> This is printed from the same setting up of the type as the quarto edition in the *Two Plays* of 1658, the pages not only being re-arranged in the frame, but the number of lines to the page being reduced from 33 to 30.   (See *Essay,* p. xii).
>
> B.M. (643. b. 43).   Bodl.   Dyce.

* The Amorous Warre.   A Tragi-Comœdy.   *Printed in the Yeare* 1648.

> B.M. (1346. c. 2).

[Another edition].   By J. M. St. of Ch. Ch. in Oxon.   *Oxford, Henry Hall, for Ric Davis.*   1659.   8vo.

> B.M. (643. b. 35).   Bodl.   Dyce.

P. 77. Middleton. *Two Plays.* 1657. The volume should contain an engraved portrait, unsigned, and a stationer's catalogue. Both are found in the copy in Mr. Huth's library.

P. 79. *A Game at Chess.* n.d. * [Another edition.]

In place of present note, *read:* This edition has the same titlepage as the above, from which it may be distinguished by having a query (?) at the end of the first line of the " Induction" in place of a semicolon (;) as is there the case, and also in the frequent use of *VV* for *W* in the speakers' names. Copies of the two editions will be found in the Dyce collection.

> B.M. (161. a. 10, last two leaves only.) Dyce.

P. 80. *The Spanish Gipsie.* 1661. ("for Kirkman.") *Add note:* Another issue, differing from the above in the imprint and stationer's advertisement at the end alone.

P. 81. *Your Five Gallants.* Sig. A–L. So Hazlitt in this *Manuel of Old English Plays* as quoted. I very much doubt its existence, however. His remarks on the subject elsewhere (H. 392, I. 289) are quite unintelligible.

Munday. *The Two Italian Gentlemen.* It is evident from the S. R. entry and from Kirkman's list that the title of the play was *Fidele and Fortunatus* (not *Fortunio* as Hazlitt and Ward have it). *The Two Italian Gentlemen* is the running title.

P. 82. Nabbes. Insert before first entry :
Playes, Masques, Epigrams, Elegies, and Epithalamiums. Collected into one Volume. By Thomas Nabbes. *I. Dawson.* 1639.

> General titlepage prefixed to a collection of the separate editions of the following plays :
>
> *Microcosmus*, 1637.
> *Hannibal and Scipio*, 1637.
> *Covent-Garden*, 1638.
>
> *Totenham-Court*, 1639.
> *The Unfortunate Mother*, 1640.
> *The Bride*, 1640.
>
> B.M. (11,775. bbb. 9.)

P. 83. Norton. *Forrex and Porrex.* n.d. Note. *Add:* The authors' names appear in the printer's preface.

P. 86. Quarles. *The Virgin Widow.* Second edition. *Add date:* 1656.

P. 87. Randolph. *Poems.* 1643. For *London.* (period), read *London* (comma).

P. 91. Rutter. *The Cid.* 1650. *For* B.M. (168. b. 22), *read* B.M. (162. b. 22).

P. 94. Shakespeare. Note that with regard to the entries of the Shakespeare folios, while I believe them to be correct so far as they go, no attempt has been made to indicate the very numerous variations which exist. This is rather a particular branch of the subject for which I must refer students to the special authorities on Shakespearian bibliography.

P. 99. *Titus Andronicus.* 1611. Prefix asterisk (*).

P. 103. Pseudo Shakespearean Plays. *Thomas Lord Cromwell.* 1602. Omit asterisk (*).

Pericles. 1609. *For* Prince. *(period), read* Prince : *(colon).*

P. 104. *Pericles.* 1609. In place of this entry, read:

[Pericles]. *Imprinted at London for Henry Gosson.* 1609.

> A different edition, but having the titlepage identical with the above. It may be distinguished by having the stage direction on A2 " Enter Gower " misprinted " Eneer Gower."

P. 106. Shirley. *Six Plays.* 1653. *Add:* 8vo.

There are two portraits of Shirley, one by Marshall and one by Gaywood, which seem to be found more or less indifferently with the present volume, the *Honoria and Mammon* of 1659, and the *Poems, &c.* of 1646 (See *Masques*). Which belongs strictly to which I cannot at present say. Hazlitt allots the Marshall to the *Poems*, the Gaywood to the other two.

Two Plays. 1657. Note. *For* edition, *read* editions.

P. 107. *The School of Complement.* 1637. The author's name again appears in full at the end of the dedication. It was omitted in 1667.

P. 110. *Honoria and Mammon.* 1659. The portrait will be found in B.M. (C. 12. f. 19 (9).)

P. 111. SIDNEY, MARY, *Countess of Pembroke.* Properly, the heading should, of course, run : HERBERT, MARY, *Countess of Pembroke (née Sidney).*

Stephens. *Cynthia's Revenge.* [Another issue]. 1613.

> The titlepage differs only in having the name inserted. A copy is in the Dyce collection. Mr. Halliwell assigned the play to John Swallow on the authority of an allusion in some of the commendatory verses, for

which he is scoffed at by Mr. Fleay. The ascription had, however, been already made by Kirkman. This must have been traditional, and borne out as it is by the reference in the verses is pretty well convincing. Probably then the issue with Stephens' name is the earlier.

P. 113. Suckling. After the *Last Remains* insert :

The Works of Sir John Suckling. Containing All his Poems, Plays, Letters, &c. Published by His Friends (from his own Copies) to perpetuate his Memory. *for Henry Herringman.* 1676.

> The separate parts, including titlepages and imprints, are mostly reprinted from earlier editions.   In the case of the plays they are as follows :
> Aglaura . . . *for Humphrey Moseley.* 1658.
> Aglaura [Act v.] . . . *for H. H.* 1672.
> The Goblins . . . *for Humphrey Moseley*, 1658.
> Brennoralt . . . *for Humphrey Moseley.* L658. [*sic.*]
> The Sad One . . . *for Humphrey Moseley.* 1659.
>
> W. W. G.

P. 114. Tatham. *The Mirror of Fancies.* 1657. *Add :* 12mo.

In Maidment and Logan's edition a copy is said to be in the B.M., but it does not appear in the Catalogue.

P. 115. Tomkis. *Albumazar.* The author of this play may with tolerable certainty be identified with John Tomkins. He was the son of Thomas Tomkins (a name for which Tomkis is probably a scribal error) and was a former scholar of Trinity.

Tourneur. *The Revengers Tragedy.* 1608. Prefix asterisk (*).

P. 118. Webster. *The Duchess of Malfi.* 1678. Prefix asterisk (*).

P. 119. *Appius and Virginia.* 1659. This is a re-issue with a new title-page only.

Wever. *Iuventus.* ("by Vele"). *Add note :* The author's name again occurs at the end of the play.

P. 120. Wilmot. *Tancred and Gismund.* 1591. *Add note :* The author's name appears at the end of the epistle dedicatory.

P. 126. *The Wars of Cyrus.* In place of reference to Heber and Hazlitt, *read :* B.M. (C. 34. b. 15).

P. 128. *Mucidorus.* After the edition of 1619 insert :

N

[Another edition.] *for Iohn Wright.* 1621.
  Municipal Lib., Danzig.

P. 129. For the whole of the *Solimon and Perseda* entry substitute the following, and note that the edition represented by B.M., 11,773. c. 11 (now C. 57. c. 15) and G. 18,612, is a forgery, printed about 1815.

The Tragedie of Solimon and Perseda. Wherein is laide open, Loues constancie, Fortunes inconstancie, and Deaths Triumphs. *Edward Allde, for Edward White.* [Colophon :] *for Edward White.* 1599. 8vo in fours.
  B.M. (C. 34. b. 45.) Bodl. Dyce.

  [Another issue.] Newly corrected and amended. *Edward Allde, for Edward White.* [Colophon :] *for Edward White.* 1599. 8vo in fours.
  The sheets of the above edition re-issued with the alteration on the titlepage.
    B.M. (161. b. 4.)

The Tragedye of Solyman and Perseda. Wherein is laide open, Loues constancy, Fortunes inconstancy, and Deaths Triumphs. *Edward Allde for Edward White.* [Colophon :] *for Edward White.* 8vo in fours.
  This is in all probability the earlier edition.
    B.M. (C. 34. b. 44.)

P. 131. *Il Pastor Fido.* 1602. Note. *For* Giovanni Battista Guarini, *read* Battista Guarini.

P. 132. *Il Pastor Fido.* "for Iohn Waterson." 1633. *Add :* 12mo.
This is evidently the earlier issue, since it was Waterson who signed the epistle dedicatory. The assignment to Shears appears, moreover, in the S.R., under date Sept. 6, 1633.

P. 134. *Lingua.* 1657. Omit T.C.C. from list of copies and insert :
  [Another issue]. A Serious Comœdy. First Acted at Trinity Colledge in Cambridge : After at the Free-School at Huntington. *for Simon Miller.* 1657. 8vo.
  Another issue of the sheets of the above, with a different titlepage.
    T.C.C.

Also in next entry read :
  [Another edition]. A pleasant Comœdie. *N. Okes for Simon Waterson.*

P. 137. *Fair Em.* n.d. The only known copy is in the Bodleian.

The Knave in Graine. 1640. After this entry insert :

Tyrannicall-Government Anatomized : or, a Discourse Concerning Evil-Councellors. Being The Life and Death of John the Baptist. And Presented to the Kings most Excellent Majesty by the Author. Die Martis, 30. Januarii, 1642. It is Ordered by the Committee of the House of Commons concerning Printing, That this Book be forthwith printed and published : Iohn White. *for John Field,* 1642.

> Translated from the Latin play *Baptistes* of G. Buchanan. Since the date of the volume is 1642-3, its omission in the *List of Plays* was perhaps hardly an error.
> B.M. (643. d. 28.)

The Ghost. 1653. After this entry insert :

The Queen, or the Excellency of her Sex. An Excellent old Play. Found out by a Person of Honour, and given to the Publisher, Alexander Goughe. *T. N., for Thomas Heath,* 1653.

> B.M. (E. 216 (4). Dated by Thomason "August 13.")

Filli di Sciro. 1655. This translation, as I have just discovered, was the work of Jonathan Sidnam, whose version of the *Pastor Fido,* alluded to in the prefatory verses, is preserved in B.M. Addit. MS., 29,493. Also note that 164. h. 2, is a better copy than 643. c. 66.

P. 138. *The London Chanticleers.* 1659. Note. *For* sold by S. M., *read* printed for Simon Miller. *Also to copies add :* B.M. (643. d. 36.)

Tom Tyler. 1661. *To copies add :* B.M. (643. d. 63.)

P. 140. *Necromantia.* Omit asterisk (*).

P. 143. Shirley. *The Duke's Mistress.* *Add date :* 1638.

Index of Authors. P. 147. col. 1. T., I. For *Gratix,* read *Gratiæ.*